Breaking the Wealth Code

How You Can Earn Your First Million & Create a Lifetime of Wealth

BREAKING THE WEALTH CODE

HOW YOU CAN EARN YOUR FIRST MILLION & CREATE A LIFETIME OF WEALTH*

JOHN HRIMNAK

Forbes Success Strategies, Inc.
Scottsdale, Arizona

FIRST EDITION

Published by **Forbes Success Strategies, Inc.**
PO Box 10549, Scottsdale, Arizona 85271-0549
(602) 919-0105

ISBN 1-58588-199-6

Breaking the Wealth Code
How You Can Earn Your First Million & Create a Lifetime of Wealth

For more information, contact: Forbes Success Strategies, Inc.
Or visit: www.breakingthewealthcode.com

Business / Personal Finance

DEDICATION

I want to dedicate this book to my two children, Madisson and Jared. They and their generation are the leaders of tomorrow and contrary to popular belief tomorrow is looking very bright. We believe tomorrow will be full of prosperity, health, joy, peace, and destiny. Americans are a people of resolve and undying commitment to freedom and our way of life. My children understand that the best way to predict their future is to create it.

I am proud of both Madisson and Jared just for being. I'm excited about their dreams and how they will help make this world a better place to live. Even at their young ages, they understand how to have money work for them through the vehicle of business ownership and investments. I look forward to how their example and leadership will influence individuals to create a life long cycle of wealth.

TABLE OF CONTENTS

ACKNOWLEDGMENTS   i

FOREWORD   1

1 IT'S A GOOD LIFE   3

2 HOW MUCH IS TOO MUCH?   13

3 THINKING FOR A CHANGE   31

4 GOALS ARE OVERRATED   49

5 THERE WILL BE PLENTY OF TIME
    TO SLEEP WHEN YOU'RE RICH   61

6 LOOKING RICH IS EXPENSIVE   71

7 WORKING FOR MONEY IS HARD WORK   87

8 PURPOSE DRIVEN WEALTH   113

9 REAL MONEY, REAL TIME WEALTH   137

10 GETTING DOWN TO BUSINESS   157

11 REAL EQUITY IN REAL ESTATE   167

12 SEE YOU AT THE TOP   185

ACKNOWLEDGMENTS

I want to first of all thank God, which in and of itself would require an entire book of its own to describe what He's done in my life. Secondly, I want to thank my wife, Shannon, for being my best friend, my greatest business partner, my soul mate and the love of my life. She has truly inspired me to success and with out her support and encouragement this book would not have been written.

I want to thank my mother, Linda, for her unchanging love and for being a constant source of inspiration and encouragement. I want to thank my in-laws, James and Leslee Testa, for making me one of their own, adopting me as part of their family and always challenging me to believe in myself.

I want to thank Dr. Carl Anderson and Dr. Maureen Anderson for adopting my family into theirs, mentoring me into an amazing life, and for their selfless commitment to changing a generation and a nation.

I want to thank all of my mentors starting with Scot Anderson for teaching me how to be a father, teaching me the value of relationships, being one of my best friends, and for being my life long universal business partner.

I want to thank Richard Taylor for teaching me the keys to cultivating relationships, sharing valuable life changing lessons, and for his unwavering support. I want to thank Jason Anderson for being a catalyst for me to dig deeper into my life in search of higher levels of excellence. I want to thank David Crammer for directing all of the key elements of this book project, being my best friend, making me laugh until I can't breathe, and for being my twin. I want to thank all of my four brothers especially Henry Sandoval for being my father figure. In addition, I want to thank Dr. Matt Mannino for all he has shared to build my businesses, for keeping my family healthy, and for being a friend.

Finally I want to thank my editing team Don Enevoldsen, Holly Sitzler, Tammy Zubeck, Shelley Johnson and Theo Bushanam for all their tireless work to ensure this book is excellent.

FOREWORD

Do you desire to become wealthy so you can spend more time with your family, make a difference in the world, or maybe to have more control over your time, life and destiny? If that is your vision of your future, search no more, Breaking the Wealth Code gives you the answer. Now you can join the ranks of the rare 2% who control the wealth of the world.

Rita Davenport said, "Money is not important, but it ranks right up there with oxygen." How well I know. I used to be so broke I'd walk past a bank and trip the alarm. Creditors would call my house and my children would tell them, "My daddy said he ain't home." Like John, I can tell you from first hand experience, poverty sucks. Former comedian Red Foxx once said, "Money can't buy you happiness, but it can make a big down payment!"

John Hrimnak has written a classic on how to create wealth. Einstein said, "Genius is the capacity to make the complicated simple." John, using practical everyday language, stories, examples, and insights, makes it possible for any individual to become wealthy.

As a speaker and author, I have read many books over the years on how to get rich. This book stands at the top of my list. John leaves no rock unturned. He makes you aware of how you can create tremendous wealth using his approach on a part-time basis. Every page will help you overcome possibility blindness, transform the way you see yourself, and change the way you view money and the role it plays in shaping your life. Breaking the Wealth Code helps you to conquer the unconscious, poverty mindset that causes most people to live in a state of lack, misery, and hard times.

This book is a roadmap that will empower you to become as Mother Theresa would say, "A pencil in the hand of God." It will help you to start writing a new chapter in your life. Breaking the Wealth Code, in its own subliminal approach, will decrease your level of impoverished thinking and increase your sense of deservingness. You will come to a place in yourself where you will give yourself permission to be wealthy. Ninety-eight percent of people go to their graves unhappy, unfulfilled, and empty not knowing there was a better way.

Many give up out of disappointment, defeat, and discouragement, feeling that it is impossible to accumulate wealth if you were not born with a silver spoon in your mouth like Donald Trump, the Rockefellers or the Kennedys. Finally, John Hrimnak has broken the wealth code and has made it possible for all of us to join the elite class of people.

LES BROWN

1
It's a Good Life

"What have you eaten today?" the nice lady dressed in an orange, plaid checkered skirt and orange blouse almost whispered. She asked in such a quiet voice that it seemed she did not want my mother or grandmother to hear the question.

My grandmother had just answered the door and went to get my mom from the backyard to tell her we had a visitor. She came in just as I was about to answer the quiet question.

My mom instantly changed the subject, almost as if she knew what had been asked and didn't want me to respond. Before I could get anything out of my mouth, she had changed the subject with a different question to the lady.

"How soon can we get our first check?" she blurted out.

I was ten at the time and I didn't think anything of it. After all, I knew exactly what I had eaten for lunch and with one hundred percent certainty, I could tell her what I would have for dinner, too. And both seemed perfectly normal.

The nice lady continued with a series of routine questions. She wanted to know all kinds of things. "How many adults and children live here?"

There were seven of us in the 600 square foot, one-bath home. That seemed normal to me, too.

"What is your diet like on a daily basis?"

My grandmother and mother dutifully explained that our regular diet was mainly beans, tortillas and milk and cereal.

Asking these questions was her job. And she had a lot of them.

"When do you expect to have the electricity back on?"

She saw that there were some parts of the house where concrete showed through the worn vinyl. In other places, there was just the pad for the carpet, the kind that moves when you walk on it. She asked if we were in the process of replacing the carpet.

We weren't.

She asked about the current mortgage and rent and how we were able to make that every month.

She asked to see the kitchen cupboards and storage areas in the refrigerator.

We started toward the kitchen when she stopped. Something caught her attention. There was a two-by-three foot hole in the wall, stuffed with paper towels. She walked over to it and looked closer.

"Why are these paper towels stuffed in here?" she asked.

My mother answered that they were there to prevent roaches from getting in.

I could have told her that it didn't work very well.

I could see them coming through all the time. And Black Widow spiders followed them in through the same hole like they were chasing them. It didn't stop them at all. That seemed pretty normal to me.

The nice lady examined the hole for a moment and then she backed up. As she did, she kicked one of the dining room chairs. This caused her to notice that two chairs were intentionally touching, facing each other.

"Why are these chairs arranged this way?"

My mom hesitated for a second, so I answered for her. "That's my bed."

I thought the nice lady would be proud of me for thinking of the idea of putting those chairs together so that I didn't have to sleep on the floor. The floor was never a fun place to be at night. You could literally feel and hear the cockroaches and their friends come out after dark. They were the large ones that could fly. And the Black Widows came out with them. I don't remember ever getting bitten by one, but I was deathly afraid of them. Putting the chairs together seemed like a great idea. Apparently the nice lady didn't think so.

"Is this where you sleep?" she asked with a horrified look on her face.

That look will never leave my memory. It shook me to the core of my being. I tried to answer but words wouldn't come out of my mouth. My lips began to quiver and I began to cry.

Suddenly, nothing seemed very normal any more. It dawned on me in that instance, from the way she reacted, that I was not normal at all, and my life wasn't normal. For the first time, I realized I was poor. I remember that moment like it was yesterday.

The lady was a social worker with the county of El Paso, Texas. My mom had called Social Services for food stamps and financial aid. Back in those days, they sent a worker to your house to check on the living conditions before they processed the request.

I guess you could say I had a rough childhood. The house was built in 1934. It was sandwiched between a commercial section and a two-bedroom attached duplex.

My grandfather owned everything at one time. When he died, he left my grandma, who helped to raise me, with a $232.00 Social Security check and the sporadic rent that the duplex next door managed to bring in. With two adults, me and four other brothers living there, money was always scarce.

I didn't grow up with a dad. He knew about me but, for reasons I did not know, he never gave any child support to my mom. In fact, I was thirteen years old before I spoke to him for the first time over the phone. It wasn't until I was thirty-six that I even saw a picture of him. It's funny how you picture someone when you've only talked to him. You get an image in your mind and that's how you picture that person when you think of him. I always imagined him looking like Pierce Brosnan. He didn't.

I grew up in the worst possible location in El Paso. It was called the Segundo Barrio which translates to "Second Ward." Poverty there was considerably below the national average, but it was the norm in that part of town.

Drugs and gang violence were a part of everyday life. We lived a half-mile away from the police head-quarters for the entire city and less than two miles from the border with Mexico. It was a rough and dangerous place. But that's all I knew so I thought everyone lived that way.

> It was a rough and dangerous place. But that's all I knew so I thought everyone lived that way.

I thought it was nor-mal except when I visited my uncle's house and sometimes spent the night. His place was only 1,200 square feet, but it seemed like a mansion to me. There was a fireplace and more than one bedroom. He even had two bathrooms. All the kids in that neighbor-hood had bikes to ride and toys to play with and when it was time to eat, I got the good stuff, and I didn't have to stop until I was full.

I didn't mind working hard. I got a paper route when I was eleven so I could make a few extra bucks. I lived for the pizza sales party that the district manag-ers took us to once a week. The El Paso Times was big business. At least it seemed that way to me. I made $10 to $12 every other week and I felt like I was doing well. That was back in the old days when the paper route deliv-ery boys had to collect from the customers. I learned sales at a very young age. I had to convince people that they needed to keep paying me so that they could continue to receive my valuable service—the newspaper.

One morning at 4:00 am, on my way out to pick up the newspapers, my mom gave me a big hug and a kiss and said she was going to be gone for a couple of weeks. My brother was already in the car, getting ready to take her.

I asked her where she was going and when she would be back. She said that she had to take care of something that had to be done and there was no other way. She said she would be back soon.

Huge tears rolled down my face. I begged her to take me with her. I promised that I would be good, and the paper route would always be there when I got back. I even told her that I didn't need to pack anything because everything I needed was already with me.

She hugged me again and kissed me on the cheek and promised she should be right back and I would never even miss her. Within a few minutes she was out the door and the car was off to the airport.

It would be a year and a half before I saw her again. When she returned, she had a new husband and my new baby brother.

There was no doubt that the odds were stacked against me. I don't share these things to impress you or to look for sympathy. Rather, I want to impress upon you that the past is exactly that—the past. It can either hold you back or it can give you purpose and a passion to create a better tomorrow.

I believe that what you focus on gets bigger. If you focus on the past and the past was bad, it will only be magnified. If you focus on the future and the good, it will grow.

It doesn't matter where you started. You can be wealthy. It doesn't matter where you grew up or how much money you have now or who your family was. You and you alone can decide to control your thoughts. If you don't control your thoughts, then your thoughts will control you. Thoughts are a lot more powerful than most people realize they are. I believe that a person's thought life really is at the core of whether or not he or she will be successful in life.

I have never taken so much time to think about and remember my childhood as I did writing this opening chapter. It was difficult to say the least. I had forgotten much of it, since I've never allowed myself to dwell on it.

I do not often allow my thoughts to take me into the dark corners of my past. In fact, the only time that I spend thinking about the past is to remind me how much I desire to live a better life, to provide my children and my family with all the love, guidance and tools for success that they need. I live a life focused on tomorrow.

For those people who have experienced a difficult past, it is important that you make the decision to begin forgetting about it by refusing to allow yourself to think about anything but the future. Get on with designing and living a great life.

Hopefully, what you just read does not apply to you. I hope you never experienced the poverty that I did or anything like it. My wife, Shannon, is certainly one of those individuals. She had a great childhood. I think that's great and it's what I would wish for everyone. But I know many people whose past is similar to mine and who need to be reminded and encouraged to move forward and not allow that past to damage or destroy their future.

Consider the past to inspire you to change for tomorrow.

I wrote this book because in the last couple of years, I have experienced a great deal of financial success and I wish someone would have shared with me much earlier the practical steps that I could have taken to begin seeing the results that I now have.

I have achieved financial independence. By applying the principles that I am sharing in this book, I believe anyone can become a millionaire in three years by working at it part time. I've lived it and done it for myself. It's about having a strategy and working smart, not hard.

Simply put, this book will give you all the tools and information you will need to earn your first million. What you do with the knowledge and how you choose to apply it is up to you.

Making your first million will certainly take hard work. It doesn't happen overnight, and it doesn't happen without some effort, contrary to what some late night commercials tell you. It takes a commitment of time every week. But in the end, it's worth it. I don't regret a single hour I spent or any sacrifice I had to make.

Of course, it's easy to say that now, but in reality, I didn't have a choice. There simply was not enough money left at the end of the month. I did not enjoy being there. From the day that I realized I was poor, I didn't like it. I hated being faced every month with "not

> **Consider the past to inspire you to change for tomorrow.**

enough." However, I can honestly say that I'm thankful I had "not enough" pushing me to succeed. I believe it's important to have strong reasons to succeed. And "not enough" is a good one.

If you're in the same situation or you bought this book because you really need to make more money, that's great. If you feel like you have enough money, then I trust that by the end of the book you will find strong empowering reasons to earn more.

Without strong enough reasons, making money is just an option. Being comfortable financially is one of the worst things I can think of because it keeps people believing that as long as they have just enough, everything will be just fine and they can sit back and enjoy life.

A lot of people are too fearful of making mistakes. So, to make sure they don't fail, they just never try. They're sure to never fail, but they are also sure to never succeed.

I can assure you that one of the reasons I am where I am today is because I've made most of the mistakes that you can possibly make on this path. People can learn either by experience or by education. I learned a lot by experience. I wish I had learned more from education much earlier. It was a much harder way to go.

But in spite of that, I have learned some very important things and perhaps the most important is the understanding that a mistake is not a mistake if you learned something from it. You can turn every mistake into something good if you let it educate you. If you never make a mistake, it only means you're not doing anything.

So I encourage you to get rid of your fear of making a mistake. Instead, move forward and start living your destiny. Wealth is not an accident and it doesn't just magically appear. Wealth is achieved by taking-real life action in a methodical format with the intention of increasing cash flow, eliminating debt and building your assets.

While there are several methods to create wealth, I can personally verify that this process truly works because it has produced results in my life. In the next few chapters we will lay a foundation before discussing the real money, real wealth building system in chapter 9. I know you want to skip right to Chapter 9 now, but don't do it. You need a strong foundation if you want to build anything meant to last. Completing this book will provide you with what you need to begin taking precise and practical action to building your own wealth.

2
How Much Is Too Much?

W e were in line at our gate at Providence Airport, waiting to board our plane. We had arrived plenty early. The flight was scheduled to leave at 10:30 in the morning. It was the end of a vacation at Cape Cod. We were ready to head home to Phoenix, a five-and-a-half-hour flight.

I love Southwest Airlines but I have to tell you, I believe they contribute to world hunger on flights longer than three hours when they have no food available other than a tiny bag of peanuts. I learned this on the flight from Phoenix to Cape Cod and I vowed that I would not starve on the return flight.

Right after we got our bags checked, I stopped at a full-service restaurant and stocked up. I got a breakfast burrito, two chicken salads, a hamburger and two club sandwiches. It was only my wife and me with our two kids, who are both quite young, but I wasn't going to take any chances. We would not have a shortage of food.

As we stood there in the line at the gate, I overheard a middle-aged couple behind me discussing how hungry they were. They noticed the three big bags of food we were carrying and they decided that maybe they should get something, too, for that long flight.

I turned around and encouraged them to do so. I didn't want to see anyone suffer the hunger that I had experienced on the flight there. "It is a long flight," I said, "and believe me, you might get a bag of peanuts, but that will be about it." I even offered to hold their place in line while they went. They thanked me and decided which one of them was going to go.

They seemed to be a very nice couple. We exchanged pleasantries and talked about the line and the flight. At one point, I turned around to talk to my son and I heard the wife say that she was going to leave for a few minutes and see what she could find to eat.

From their appearance, they seemed to be upper-middle class. Nothing indicated that they were lacking money. She had nice jewelry. He had a Montblanc pen sticking out of his dress shirt.

This is why it surprised me when a few minutes later, she returned empty-handed and visibly upset. She complained to her husband about how high the prices were at the airport.

"I won't pay $8.00 for a sandwich," she asserted. "It's a total rip-off, what these places at the airport get away with."

Her husband seemed to be upset about not having any food but he ended up agreeing with her and so they stood in line, already hungry but with nothing to eat.

I almost asked them, "How much is too much for a sandwich? Here, I'll make up the difference. Or better yet, here's a $20.00 bill if you're that limited in cash. Get yourself something to eat."

Why would anyone set out on a mission for food that they both wanted, knowing that it would be six or seven hours before they would have another opportunity to find any, and then return empty-handed because it was a few dollars more than they expected? It seemed absolutely ludicrous to me to suffer that much for the sake of a few dollars. It perplexed me at first, then confused me and finally annoyed me that anyone would use that reasoning.

It made no sense to me. From my perspective, it was a simple matter. I'm hungry; I'm eating. End of story. I understand that if there's not enough money then you have to be frugal but that was clearly not the case with this couple. I even considered for a moment the possibility that I could wait until we were on the plane and I could sell them my $8.00 sandwich for $20.00, once they were really starving.

We boarded the plane and as luck would have it, they ended up sitting directly behind us. For the next five and a half hours they had to sit there and watch us eat all the food we brought on board with us. At times, I could overhear them remarking about how hungry they were and how much they wished that they had brought some food. To make matters even worse, the flight attendant announced that someone on board had a peanut allergy and so they decided not to even serve the peanuts. It must have been a very long flight for that couple.

I tell you this story in order to illustrate the importance of your beliefs and how they can affect your life.

That couple had plenty of money but their belief system was one of poverty. It was not a belief system of abundance or wealth.

I realize that I may be a bit presumptuous in my assessment of them based on such a short time, but the chances are that they had other issues where money was concerned. What I saw in that small incident illustrated a belief that undoubtedly had consequences in much bigger issues. The woman took the action to go buy food but her belief system said that she shouldn't spend that much on a sandwich. The result was that she and her husband went hungry. It's not complicated.

We will talk about your actions in later chapters but before we get there, we have to start with your intentions, which are your belief systems. What you believe about money has everything to do with how much you will eventually have.

There are entire books and lengthy studies that deal with the power of your belief systems. Because we are only devoting a single chapter to it, I can only address a small amount of this information specifically as it pertains to gaining wealth and money in general. But it is vitally important so I ask you to keep an open mind, especially if this is the first time you have considered it.

Until you change your belief system, you may not be able to succeed in the "how tos." No matter what you may do to accumulate wealth, if you don't believe you deserve to keep it, then your belief system will take over and get you back to ground zero. How-tos really won't matter if you haven't changed your belief system first. It's no different than changing your belief and then never implementing the practical application to see the real change.

Your beliefs start as you are growing up. The things you were told or heard about money and finances began to take root in your mind and unless you decided at some point in your life to specifically change them, they're still in there.

> **What you believe about money has everything to do with how much you will eventually have.**

This may not seem all that bad at first. Partly, it is because you are so used to the belief systems you have that you think of it as normal and right. After all, you've never believed any other way.

However, what most people are not aware of is that those beliefs are literally running their lives. In fact, there has been a lot of research done that shows people do not consciously make 75% of their decisions. Instead, their internal beliefs make the decisions automatically without any conscious thought about it or evaluation of the issue. The belief says, "No, we can't afford that," or "No, I'm not entitled to that," or "That business and investment are too risky and I might lose." You think you are making a decision but the decision is based on the beliefs inside of you, not the information in front of you. That's a pretty scary thought if you ask me.

Other research indicates that the majority of the beliefs you hold as an adult about almost everything were formed before you were ten years old. Our beliefs are so much a part of everyday life that for the most part, we are totally unaware of them.

I like to think of them as our auto pilot system. As we are flying along on our way to our destination, we engage auto pilot and our lives are being influenced unconsciously by the inner beliefs that we hold.

We don't get to turn off the auto pilot, either. It just keeps working. The only thing we can do is to make sure we have the kinds of beliefs that will result in decisions consistent with the kind of life we want to live.

A client and friend of mine, Brian Klemmer, has built his whole company with a mission to change people's belief systems. He's been quite successful speaking across the country and holding weekend seminars. During the seminars, he compares our belief systems with a person wearing sunglasses. The sunglasses symbolize a person's beliefs. They change how that person sees the world.

To illustrate this, he gives one participant in the audience a pair of green sunglasses and another a pair of blue ones. He then asks them to describe various items in the room, including the color.

It drives the point home when you see that no matter how much you might disagree with someone when he says that everything in the room is green, as long as he keeps green sunglasses on, he will never see any other color. You might emphatically try to convince him that the object is some other color, but he will still see it as green.

Your belief system works the same way. If what you believe about money is that being rich means you have no friends and that you always have a lot of problems, then no matter what kind of goals you set, you will have a battle going on inside of you. You consciously say that you want to gain wealth, but your belief system tells you that wealth is a bad thing because it will make you unhappy with all your problems and you'll have no friends. And when the battle is over, you will sabotage your own goals. You will unconsciously find a way to keep from having the wealth.

So what do you believe about money? It might not be as clear as you think.

Let's go through some questions that will help you discover your true beliefs. As you ask yourself these questions, be completely honest. And if you think you believe even a part of the statement, make a circle around it so you will know what to work on when we talk about how to change your beliefs. Be as true and honest with yourself as possible. After all, it's about changing your beliefs, not someone else's. Denying them won't accomplish anything.

Before we get started, here is another concept that you may not have thought about before. I believe that most people have a value that they unconsciously attach to money. They see it as either good or bad. But money is neutral. It is not good or bad. It's what you do with money that determines its value.

If you had $100,000 and you invested it in real estate and in a business and then took the profits from both and used them to improve the quality of life for your family, you would probably agree that the money was good.

However, if you had the same $100,000 and you used it to purchase illegal drugs with the intention of re-selling them, and you began to profit from the sales to end users, then I think most of us would agree that it was bad money.

The outcome and the perception of the money's value are directly connected to what it was used for. It was the same $100,000 in both illustrations but what it was used for determined in our minds what it became. The actual $100,000 is really just a tool to use for whatever you choose to use it for. The money itself is neutral.

Money can be used to promote terrorism around the world or the same money can be used to fight terrorism. Money is nothing more than paper. What value we assign to its outcome and purpose in life is our own choice. Ask yourself these questions.

- Do you believe money is bad?
- Do you believe you being wealthy is wrong?
- Do you believe having more money than you need is necessary?
- Do you believe if you become rich that you will be liked among friends and family?
- Do you believe that building wealth is too difficult or impossible?
- Do you believe all you need is a lucky break to be rich?

- Do you believe that you deserve to be wealthy?
- Do you believe that having a lot of money creates a lot of problems?
- Do you believe you are worthy of having nice things in life?
- Do you believe your family deserves a higher quality of life?
- Do you believe you are not very good with money and finances?
- Do you believe everyone will want something from you if you became rich?
- Do you believe you will have to give up a lot in order to gain wealth?
- Do you believe it takes money to make money?
- Do you believe you are smart enough to become rich?
- Do you believe it's acceptable for you to be wealthy in spite of others close to you that may not have enough money?
- Do you believe you are so comfortable that you don't need to create wealth?
- Do you believe that working a good job is enough in life?
- Do you believe that rich people did something that was illegal to earn their money?
- Do you believe money is not important?
- Do you believe you will be stressed out as you create wealth?
- Do you believe all debt is bad?

- Do you believe you need more time before starting to build wealth?
- Do you believe becoming rich will change you
  for the worse?

Now for a Change

In case you were wondering if you really believed
some of the statements that you just read, the reality is that
your results equal your intentions or your true beliefs. Your
results and your beliefs/intentions are one and the same in
that you ultimately will only do what you really believe.

As strange and foreign as this might sound, it is
completely true. You are where you are in life right now
because of your beliefs. You have the results that you
have right now because of what you have believed in the
past; what you believed you should or shouldn't have.

I realize that this information may not excite you,
but don't put the book down yet. Let's get started understanding how to change your beliefs. Discovering and ad-
mitting that you have any beliefs that are in disagreement
with where you really want to go and what you want to
achieve in life will now give you the opportunity to correct them.

As we begin to discuss how to change your belief
system, let's start with some popular cures that are out
there. A lot of different seminars and authors teach some
pretty weird things about belief systems.

First, some believe that if you had a horrible childhood, you must have been programmed with some really

bad beliefs about you and your life. Those people think that you would need to enroll in counseling for ten years to change all those things. And most of the time, they conveniently happen to have a counseling service available for a nominal price.

I realize that in some cases of severe abuse and other traumatizing events, counseling is important. However, for the most part, it's just a decision to get over the past and move on as I discussed in Chapter 1. Counseling has its place and there is value in it, but I'm not in agreement with those who say that it is a requirement for any lasting and meaningful change.

> **Your results and your beliefs/intentions are one and the same in that you ultimately will only do what you really believe.**

In addition to the counseling proponents, there are other seminars and classes that insist you will never achieve anything great or accomplish your goals until you enroll in their expensive seminars to undergo surgery on your belief system.

I've attended some of these seminars and have benefited from a few. One in particular, I recommend is "Beyond Wealth" presented by sourcetrainings.com. I believe that far more people fail to take action than people who take action and fail. Don't depend on seminars to do all the work for you. Instead, focus on changing any wrong belief systems that may still hinder you from experiencing success.

I know that for me, it was simply a matter of starting to do whatever I could to earn extra money and along the way, I discovered some of the limiting beliefs that I had. When I realized I had a belief in me that was not consistent with my values or my goals, I simply made a decision to replace it with something else.

For example, a year ago I started a hobby of buying and selling sports cars. I started with relatively less expensive makes and models. After a while, I decided to buy a Porsche, which I always wanted at some point in my life.

It was the best day in my life when I found a private owner and met him at my bank to buy it. It was only a few years old and still had the manufacturer's warranty. I was so excited I didn't even bother to test drive it. I saw it and my mind was made up. I bought it on the spot with a cashier's check. Everything was awesome. I was on Cloud Nine for a couple of weeks.

Then something strange happened. All of a sudden, I felt guilty for having it. I started feeling like I had no business even owning a Porsche. I could have done so many other things with the money. I could have invested it to make more money or given it to my church or something. Who was I to spend that much on a car?

This went on for a couple of weeks and finally, as I discussed it with my wife, Shannon, it occurred to both of us that it stemmed from the guilt I felt because of the rest of my family. They could barely afford two car payments and this was my fifth car, the one that I only used on the weekends. My belief at that time was that it was not right for me to enjoy such an extravagant car for a few hours a week when my extended family needed money.

Of course, I did help my family whenever I knew they needed anything, especially my mom. In fact, a few months before, I had shown up at her house with a debt-free car for her. So I knew that I actually was helping and sharing with my family. But for some reason, this was the belief that was causing me to feel so much guilt.

Sometimes your true belief systems may not make any sense. Sometimes you have no idea why you feel a certain way. But those beliefs, no matter how irrational, will affect your behavior and your success.

The solution was simple. I told myself, "I work hard. I deserve whatever vehicle I want and can rightfully afford and own. It is not a bad thing." I added this new belief that unless I experience abundance for myself, I will not be in a position to ever share with my family and friends.

The old belief that said I shouldn't have the car in the first place would have kept me from striving to achieve other financial goals. Rather than let it do that, I added a new goal to our list. I would purchase a similar vehicle for my in-laws to reinforce my new belief. The new belief would be more powerful than the old one. (By the way, my in-laws don't know this yet unless they're reading this book or one of you tells them. So let's keep it a surprise. I'm probably a year or so from achieving that goal.)

I changed the limiting belief that was making me feel guilty into one that said unless I have too much, I can't give to others. My new belief was fueled with the desire and goal to give. I'm sure there are some other ways of replacing this bad belief with a better one, but this one made sense and seemed like the right alternative. The real issue is that there is no one right solution for your limiting belief. Just get one that makes sense to you and use it to empower your future success.

Now let's get down to talking about how we change limiting beliefs. First, take a look at the belief and realize that it is not grounded in reality. For example, take the belief, "Money is bad because it causes stress and will eventually kill you." In reality that's not really true. If it were true, why do you work forty to sixty hours a week for something that will kill you?

Here's another one: "It takes money to make money." If that is true, then how do you explain some of the most successful and wealthy people who started with nothing and became very wealthy? This belief is really based on fear. It causes a person to never do anything because he really never has enough money to start and he never will because he believes it takes money, which he doesn't have, to make money. How crazy is that? The reality is that it takes ideas to make money. I will prove this belief in later chapters.

The second thing to do in changing limiting beliefs is to create an alternative belief that is relevant and choose that belief instead. For example, let's examine the belief, "I'm not very good with money." I would consider replacing this belief with a new one that says, "Money and money management is a learned skill that I can understand after reading a couple of books or hiring an accountant or bookkeeper to help me with it."

Here's another example. "If I become wealthy, everyone will want something from me." I would consider replacing this belief with a new one that says, "I want to become wealthy so I can provide a great life for my family and give to my friends and charities because I have it to give."

> Create an alternative belief that is relevant and choose that belief instead.

Third, take some sort of action that empowers your new belief. This makes it real and active in your life. It may take a while before this new belief becomes a part of who you really are but that's okay. Keep exercising the new one just like you would a muscle.

After creating the new belief about having a Porsche, I not only created a goal of buying a car for my in-laws, but I also sent my mom a decent sum of money for no reason or occasion other than to enforce and activate my new belief that unless I had too much, I was not able to give to the people in my life who were important to me. Those actions empowered the belief.

So let's put it all together. Let's say that you realize that you believe you will never be wealthy, either because you grew up poor or for some other reason. Realize that this belief doesn't make rational sense in your life. The truth is that you truly desire to do great things and provide a greater level of life for your family. And there is no logical reason why you can't. That is the first step.

The second step is to replace it with a better belief. Perhaps you consciously tell yourself, "I believe that as I learn to earn extra money, I can then reinvest that to create even more money, which will lead me to wealth."

Third, take some sort of action on this belief that will empower it in your life. That might be as simple as buying this book or one similar to it that will provide you with the tools required to start earning extra money.

On the surface, I titled this chapter "How Much is Too Much?" because of the story of the couple at the airport and my interest to know just how much is too much for something that you really want. The driving force behind the title, however is to bring you to the point of asking yourself how much is too much in your own life? Is having $50,000 in your bank account too much? Is it enough for you to stop working towards earning more money?

It is a very interesting and deep question on so many levels. At what point in life are you satisfied in every area—in your relationships, at your current weight, your current income? I know that for me, just three years ago, having $50,000 in my bank account just sitting there was too much. I couldn't see it and it was more money than I ever had in a savings account in my life. The most

I had ever been able to accumulate was $3,000. And at the time, I felt like I was very well off.

Of course, now my answer to how much is too much is way beyond $50,000 in my account. How about you? What can you see yourself having? Understand that part of it is a process of financial growth. The more wealth you begin to accumulate, the more you can begin to see yourself having.

However, there is a lot to be said for being able to see it before you have it. Please take a few minutes before going on and answer these questions for yourself.

- How much money in a bank account is too much?
- How much income a year is too much?
- How much money is too much to leave as an inheritance for your children?
- How many properties are too many to own?
- How much giving is too much for you to give every year to your preferred charities?
- How much is too much to spend on a family vacation to create family memories?
- How much is too much to pay for that car you've always wanted?
- How much is too much to buy the house of your dreams?

How you answer these questions will tell you a lot about your belief system. In the next two chapters, we will continue to go a little deeper into your intentions. For the most part, you do what you believe. What you believe is something you need to be committed to checking on regularly. Make it a point to visit this chapter in the future and continue to ask yourself where you want to be compared to where you are now, and then ask yourself what action you can take to get you there.

3
THINKING FOR A CHANGE

"I am going to wait for home prices to come down a little more before I buy my first home," said my friend.

We were playing a game of pool at my house. I've known him since we were fifteen years old. We were now in our thirties. He had gotten married just a couple of years after me, and we were still very good friends.

I had just asked him when he was planning to buy his first home and if he needed help with his down payment. We were good enough friends that I felt bad that he still didn't own his own home. His comment was a response to that question.

I teased him a little and said, "Well, if what you said is true and the prices come down on homes, I'll buy another couple myself and join you."

It wasn't the first time that we discussed real estate. And it wasn't the first time I had tried to convince him to purchase a home so that he could benefit from the appreciation. But my efforts never seemed to work, no matter what I said or tried to do to convince him.

What started the conversation was something we did earlier that day. I had purchased a Hummer about a week before, something that I had been wanting for a long time. It was Labor Day and we had a lot of friends and family over. When my friend and his wife arrived that day, I greeted him at the front door, and he asked to see the new Hummer. He had been excited to take a drive in it from the moment I told him about it.

We excused ourselves from the gathering and made our way to the garage to take a spin around the block. He loved the ride and the feel. In his exuberance, he asked me how in the world I was able to afford it.

I told him that I had just sold one of my properties and had decided to use some of the proceeds from the sale. I used the profits from real estate to purchase the Hummer outright. I thought that bit of news might make a good opportunity to try again to drive the point home that it was in his best interest to buy his first home right away and not to delay any further. I was in a position to help him and I wanted to, just to get him started.

He began to talk about articles that he had seen over the past several months that said the real estate market was starting to crash. He said that there was going to be a bubble. To his way of thinking, he was concerned about what he may lose and he was convinced that the crash had already started.

I asked some questions about where he obtained his information. I encouraged him to be financially literate and make his decision based on doing research. Articles are great, especially if they provide numbers and actual statistics. I explained to him how I put the numbers together to make decisions based on financial literacy. Predictions not based on actual numbers are just mere opinions and it's important that he made good decisions based on reality.

In fact, if there was any time to purchase a home, this would certainly be it. I explained that buying a home in a down or slow market would give him more advantages because it would be a buyer's market.

We talked about it for about half an hour, and I finally gave up. We both agreed that time would tell.

Well, time did tell and several months later, he wished he had listened to me. I had done very well on the properties I had bought and sold over the past several months and he realized that he had made a mistake by waiting. Instead of making money, he had made someone else's mortgage payment by renting his home.

> **It wasn't a matter of who was right or wrong, but it was about being open to all the information.**

It wasn't a matter of who was right or wrong, but it was about being open to all the information by researching properly and making an educated decision on the facts. The market had, in fact, slowed down a little with a lot of homes on the market. However, I continued to purchase in the right locations and for the right price.

It really is true what they say is the number one rule of real estate: Location! Location! Location! Well-situated central areas of the city continued to post smaller appreciation gains while outer areas experienced slight declines of appreciation. And those who continued to invest with strategy and focus continued to increase their net worth.

My friend was held back from making money by the way he was thinking. He focused his thoughts on the risk, the economy, the market and what he saw as the future which persuaded him to make no changes and play it safe.

In the previous chapter we discussed the importance of and the impact people's belief systems can have on their lives. Closely related to how people believe is how they think.

Certainly it can be said that some of what you think comes from what you believe. However, we will focus on how external factors, like the people who are around us and those closest to us, our experiences and what we focus our attention on, all impact and affect what and how we think.

A time-tested and proven saying from the book of Proverbs, a part of the best-selling book in history, the Bible, says, "As a person thinks, so is he." This means that you become and are becoming like what you think about most of the time.

I'm not saying that if you think about a piece of chocolate cake long enough, you will become one. But I do believe that your thoughts cause you to make decisions that forever alter your life and further create what future your thoughts will dictate.

Numerous books, such as *Think and Grow Rich* by Napoleon Hill, have as their central point the value and importance of a person's thoughts. Your thoughts are a powerful force.

For example, have you ever watched a commercial on TV and seen your favorite dessert or snack and had your mouth start to salivate or start to feel pangs of hunger? We call them cravings but they originated with a thought which communicated to the rest of your body that you wanted it and needed it and told your mouth to get ready because you were about to eat it. That is why your mouth was producing the additional saliva which it was going to need if you really were about to bite into it. Your thoughts cannot differentiate between reality and fiction as you think about it and imagine it.

Do you remember watching a scary movie and being scared, feeling tense, and breathing heavily while your heart began to beat a mile a minute? What caused that? You were not the one about to be slaughtered by the bad guy, but your mind communicated to the rest of your body that it was happening to you, too. Which is why you had those physical reactions. Your thoughts are active and they are powerful.

You know, it takes just as much effort and energy to think about good things and positive outcomes as it does bad things and negative outcomes. It takes discipline to get yourself to think about situations and circumstances resulting in a positive outcome. For some, it's easier than others, depending on their thought patterns for the past several years. Some people already spend most of their time thinking about positive things instead of negative things. Others are just the opposite.

For example, imagine your next job interview going well and you getting that job. Imagine your investment making you money. Imagine yourself living the kind of life you've always dreamed of.

Without getting too deep into the science and facts behind your thought life, I want you to realize that by thinking these things, you are imagining yourself doing them and at that moment, you are affecting your beliefs about how that situation will turn out.

You might not in reality get the job, however, if you are imagining a great interview and you are believing it, you will, in fact, experience one. Then the chances of getting the job are vastly improved compared to the times you have thought the opposite and things did not turn out too well. If you dwell on the negative, your mind now begins to imagine all the things that could go wrong and most of the time, if you can remember correctly, your imagination was not so far off from how things really turned out. Murphy's Law says that if something can go wrong, it will. People who believe Murphy's Law constantly rehearse this in their minds, so they are not surprised when things do go wrong.

I'll be the first to admit that things sometimes go wrong in my life. But I'm surprised when they do. Why is that? Because I have thought and imagined that situation going right several times in my mind, not only preparing myself for it but also affecting what I believe about it. And the vast majority of the time, things turn out the way I believe I want them to. I believe and rehearse the opposite of Murphy's Law in my mind. I think everything will go right and if anything does go wrong, it won't make a difference in the situation.

> **If you dwell on the negative, your mind now begins to imagine all the things that could go wrong.**

It's up to you how you continue to choose to think about upcoming situations in life. Since you have a choice, you might as well choose to think about and imagine that things will go well and then be surprised if they don't. It doesn't surprise me when I talk with people who are expecting for things to go wrong in their lives and things actually do go wrong. By making a decision about the situation in advance, they create a self-fulfilling prophecy.

As I am writing this chapter, I am currently involved in a situation that involves two of my key clients. I brought them together for a transaction that ended up not going so great. One decided not to perform on his commitment and took a legal way out of the contract, which placed me in an awkward situation with the other client.

Without sharing all of the details, the point I'm making is that I could be pretty distracted at the moment and not be able to continue on with the things I need to do. I have already met with both individuals and dealt with the situation as best I could and there is nothing more that I can do. I am believing and imagining everything will be fine with them and with my business relationship with them individually. But I realize that there's no guarantee beyond the action I've already taken. My choosing to worry about it or be concerned about it is not going to change what happened or the outcome of what will eventually happen. All that would do is cause me to be even more concerned and upset about the whole thing.

Instead, I got up early this morning and said to myself, "Whatever they decide to do, whether it is being upset with me or continuing with me on future business opportunities, is not up to me. They have the power to decide, so why should I waste another couple of days thinking about it and worrying about the worst possible outcome?"

All the worry is simply not worth the effort. Do all that you know to do and prepare as much as humanly possible and when you are done, choose to think about a great outcome and think only positive thoughts about the situation.

In addition to what we have just discussed, choosing to worry about things instead of believing things will turn out just fine produces stress and anxiety in your life. I hate the feeling I get when I'm worried and concerned about a situation. My heart beats faster, I draw shorter breaths and I have a sick feeling in my stomach. I can't imagine any of these things being healthy for my body. I was a professional worrier at one time because I didn't understand the power that my thinking had over my life.

Understanding and learning more about what and how you think is absolutely critical to achieving your goals. In fact, where you are today is the collection of the thoughts you had yesterday. And where you go tomorrow is based on your thoughts today. If you begin to think like a wealthy person, you will, over a period of time, make choices and decisions similar to those of wealthy people, which, in turn, will produce the same results in your life that they experience in theirs. Because you have complete control of your thoughts, you are in possession of one of the key abilities to create wealth in your life. Your thoughts do not think you. You think your thoughts.

With that in mind, let's look for a moment at just how wealthy people do think. There are some basic concepts that they adhere to in the way they think about money and business that are very different from the average person.

The average person thinks of money as a way of buying nice stuff and upgrading their lifestyle with a new car or a bigger house. It's something that they will show off in an attempt to make others think or believe that they are richer and more successful than they are. They really don't see much beyond the immediate future. They want things right now instead of planning for the future.

Wealthy people, on the other hand, think more about the future than the present. They see money as a tool to create more money. Rather than being the goal, it is a means to the goal. And the goal is a secure future. They enjoy the things that common people want—new cars and nice houses—but those things are not the only thing they are interested in. They direct their thoughts toward increasing their money first and enjoying the benefits later.

Wealthy people think of investing to create a life of abundance. They think of investing as a must in order to prepare for future opportunities. They are always looking for opportunities and are not afraid to take advantage of them when they appear.

Average people think of investing as something that they can do later, after they've bought the things that they want—the new car and the nice house. Consequently, they don't have anything left to use for investment when the opportunities arrive. Instead of thinking of investment as a way to provide a life of abundance, they see it as a way to have enough for retirement.

Wealthy people think of a job as a means of getting enough money to invest. They do not commit their entire lives to a job. Instead they see it as a means to an end. With every paycheck that they get, they set aside money to use for investment.

Average people think of their job as a way to live comfortably. When they get a paycheck, they pay bills and they buy things that they want. Investment is always something that they will do later when they have more money. Of course, they never have more money because they spend it as soon as they get it.

The truth is that jobs don't provide financial se- curity anymore. And it's even more rare to find a job that will make you truly wealthy. Without learning to invest and disciplining yourself to set aside money for investment, you will never have a very secure financial foundation.

Wealthy people believe that if you don't take some risks, you have already failed. Playing it safe will keep you from ever making any kind of investment. You have to take some chances. You have to put some money into something that has the chance of multiplying. You won't make money on real estate if you don't take a risk and buy something. Wealthy people

> **Wealthy people think of time as their most valuable asset.**

know that sometimes things go wrong. But they also realize that if you don't take the chance, you will never succeed. That doesn't mean that you blindly leap into things. You have to do your homework and figure out how the investment works. The key is to take calculated risks.

Average people are afraid to take risks. All they can think about is what will happen if it doesn't work out. As a result, they never have the kind of life that they would like. They never take any risks and as a result, there is never any change in where they are. They continue at the same level for their entire lives.

Wealthy people think of time as their most valuable asset. They don't waste time on things that are not productive. They are constantly looking for ways to make every minute count. At the very least, they will spend time educating themselves in how to increase their wealth so that they are always prepared for opportunities.

Average people think of time as something to relax with. They constantly look at the time clock, waiting for work to be over so they can go home and relax. They usually think about their hobbies and interests. Enjoyment comes first in their thinking.

Wealthy people do what they need to do before they do what they want to do. There is a discipline that goes with thinking wealthy. Average people do what they want to do first and delay or avoid doing what they need to do.

Wealthy people think of personal development as a requirement to their success and growth. They constantly try to improve themselves. They read far more than the average person. They take the time to learn whenever they can. They are always looking for fresh knowledge and insight that they can put to work in their lives.

Average people think of personal development as an option that is a nice thing to do but they usually can't find the time to do much about it. It's always something that they think they will do later, when they have more time.

Investment doesn't just mean putting money into real estate or a business. It also means investing in yourself. Investing in you is the single most important thing you can do. It will help you overcome limiting beliefs, thoughts and habits. It will empower you to make easy, practical changes in your life. It will cause you to visualize a brighter future for yourself and your family.

Wealthy people just think differently. If you tell a wealthy person that the statistics say nine out of ten businesses fail, he will respond by saying that to succeed, all he has to do is start ten businesses. If you tell the same thing to an average person, he will tell you that he has a 90% chance of failing. He will ask, "What if it doesn't work?" The wealthy person will start looking for ways to make it work.

Wealthy people find out what they need to do to be successful and they just do it. They simply plan on getting it done, no matter what the price is.

We've talked quite a bit about your thoughts and some of the effects that they have. Now let's spend a few minutes talking about how to reprogram your thinking. Your thoughts drive and program your way of thinking. But if you can have a way of thinking that lines up with what you want out of life, you can completely change your life.

Think for a minute about how many people you speak with throughout your day. Depending on what you do, this can be a lot or a few. However, the most important conversation you have during the day is with yourself, that is, in the thoughts you have with yourself. We hear our thoughts and they affect and create our thinking patterns that then determine what we do about money, investments and money-making opportunities.

If you want to make a change in how you think, you need to start with the relationships in your life, your experiences and what information you allow yourself to be influenced by. First of all, I truly believe that you are the culmination of the people you hang out with the most. The people closest to you and those you spend the greatest amount of time with will ultimately determine the kinds of thoughts you have toward life. Specifically in the area of money, you will tend to think the way they do about money, business, risk and investments. It's simply human nature.

So if you're not where you want to be financially, you need to evaluate your relationships. When I did this in my life, it didn't mean I was no longer friends with certain people. However, I tried surrounding myself with people who knew more about money or had more money than I did. They thought differently about money than I did and when I was with my other friends, I made sure to be extra careful not to allow what they thought about money and anything associated with it to become a part of what I thought.

It took drawing a line in the sand, so to speak. If you don't know anybody who knows more about money than you, then buy some books and fill your mind that way. In the right books, you will begin to realize how the wealthy think and you yourself will begin to think in similar ways over a period of time.

Second, our life experiences have a lot to do with how we think. I personally struggled quite a bit with money after I was first married. We worked long, hard hours in real estate at the beginning and never seemed to get ahead in life. My wife and I worked over eighty hours every week for six years and still weren't where we wanted to be.

Of course, now I can look back and see quite a few things we were doing wrong and that I have changed since, but at the time, it just seemed like nothing would ever work for me to create massive wealth. I thought I would always be broke.

By the way, I want you to know that being broke is a state of mind and is a matter of

> **Our life experiences have a lot to do with how we think.**

living outside your means. I know a lot of people who are broke even though they have great income. They are this way because of how they think and because they spend more than they earn. I know people who earn $75,000 a year and yet they spend $80,000 and they're broke at a different income level. I also know people who make $35,000 a year, spend $20,000 of it and don't feel broke because they have extra. They are in the process of creating a great future and wealth over time. Everyone starts somewhere.

During that period of time, however, I felt broke. I began to allow myself to think average, to think that I would always be just lower middle class, no matter what. After all, that was my experience. I lived it and it was happening to me, so no one could tell me that I was having a different reality. It was my life and it was very real to me. It didn't look like it was going to change anytime soon.

What I didn't realize was that the more I thought a certain way, the more I became what I thought. The principle here is that your current or past experiences are just that. While you have personally experienced them, that does not mean they will continue to be your future. Your past does not equal your future. I wasn't reading any books back then. I wasn't working smart. I wasn't working on my beliefs or thoughts. I was just working hard.

Applying the right strategies to any career will produce great results. Your experiences, like mine, may simply have the wrong ingredients. That's all. Don't make the mistake of thinking that just because you haven't been able to create wealth you will never be able to. With the right tools, you can and you will. Creating wealth is not just an option. It is the product of the right ingredients. Now that I am aware of all the right ingredients, I have a great life.

Third, what information do you surround yourself with? What are your sources of information? As I had previously stated, articles are good and for the most part include actual numbers or statistics.

Choose carefully. Do your research and act upon the facts, not on someone else's interpretation of the facts. Be extremely careful when articles and people are trying to warn you about losing money. Look at the numbers yourself. And make the best decision based on the facts. Everyone has an opinion and I personally am not interested in hearing them most of the time.

The friend I described at the beginning of this chapter is still in the same position primarily because of how he thinks. In reality, he could have been making great money all along. Whether it was a fast-paced or slow-paced market didn't matter. It just required different strategies.

4
GOALS ARE OVERRATED

The word goal has been so overused in our society. It seems that every seminar and workshop talks about them. There are hundreds of books about them. Every January, half the world talks about them. We know them as New Year's Resolutions. On any given day on any magazine rack, you will find an article about setting your goals.

Some say the power behind them is in writing them down. Others say the power behind them is in believing them. And yet others say the power behind them is in memorizing them. Still others say other aspects are more important. It's easy to get confused.

How many times have you written your goals down somewhere and literally forgotten where you left them? Or placed them in a prominent place in your home or office and initially paid attention to them because they were new at the time, and maybe even recited them for a couple of weeks? But inevitably, after the first couple of months, you became complacent and devoted less and less attention and focus to them. Eventually you never looked at them again until it was time to update them around the first of the year. I'll admit that I have.

Your boss, a seminar teacher or someone else tells you that you need to have goals. So you just write them down and maybe they happen, but few people ever tell you how they actually come into reality.

I did this time and time again over the last fifteen years and they never really did much for me other than make me feel guilty when I realized I didn't achieve them. I believe goals are overrated and overstated when they are not fully explained. The power in goal setting and accomplishing those goals is not simply having them for the sake of having them. Just being able to say you have some goals does not necessarily mean you will ever accomplish them.

There's nothing I hate more than when someone tells me to do something and leaves out how to do it as part of the message. I'm sure you're with me when I say, if something doesn't work after a few times and there's no hope in the foreseeable future, then I'm not too excited about repeating the process.

Goals as they were taught, and for the most part, continue to be taught, are both outdated and ineffective. People mean well but they just leave out the "how" part of getting the goals to work. I believe this happens because most people do not completely understand how to unlock the creative power and force that goals really contain in it's genetic makeup.

I've asked people what their financial goals are and the most common response I get is to describe just getting by and then to declare what their next major purchase is going to be. Buying stuff and getting by are not ever going to get anyone ahead. They might give a false feeling of security and success, but people like this are just leasing their lifestyle instead of owning it. Their lifestyle will someday have to be traded down for a lesser one if they didn't build their wealth first. By contrast, wealthy people allow their wealth to drive their lifestyle.

Average people will continue in this direction until the day they realize that they spend more than they earn and have no investments or assets working for them. Living life with no goals is like setting out on a trip without a map, just leaving with no destination. My question is, how do they ever know when they have arrived if they never decided where they were headed?

> **Just being able to say you have some goals does not necessarily mean you will ever accomplish them.**

Living life with no goals is living a life with no plans or purposes. It's not a surprise that so many people hate their current jobs because they can't see beyond today and reach for a better tomorrow. I personally would rather live life believing it was going to get better and that someday I would have a better life than I have today. Even if I never accomplished those goals, at least I lived believing I would. At the very least, it would have provided me some purpose and drive to look forward to a better tomorrow.

Average people are controlled by the fear of failure. It feels so much easier never to set your sights on something greater or better in life because, what happens if you fail? Then what will your friends and family say about you after they all knew you were working towards that and didn't get there?

The most common reason people criticize others when they fail is because they don't want to be left behind. They are not doing anything to better their lives or finances, so why should you try and do something? They want to get you to believe that it will never work before you even get started believing that you can do it.

The majority of people are activity driven, whether it's in their job, in parenting or in their finances. If you were to ask people what his or her goal is for getting a raise, the overwhelming percentage would not have an answer. Instead, he or she would respond by telling you all the details and tasks that make up his or her job. They would tell you about the outstanding projects and upcoming assignments but would not be able to describe to you in any great detail their true career-related goals.

It's the same situation for most families. Parents can't describe their goals concerning their marriage or their children. They can tell you when soccer practice is or when tutoring is or when they eat dinner, but they can't tell you where they see themselves in a year or in five years. Life just gets in the way.

It's easy to have this happen. It is very easy to let society dictate what activities will keep us busy. Activity can make you feel like you are accomplishing something and even can delude you into thinking that you are pursuing your goals. However, there is a huge difference between focused activity and random activity. Focused activity brings focused and expected results. Seeing your goal through the focused activity and game plan causes it to be achievable.

Without a doubt, the number one reason that goals are not realized is due to the fact that they are not set to be achievable. They are not achievable because there is not a corresponding action plan, or the goals are simply too great to accomplish in the time frame in which they were set.

Decide on a goal and then see what it will take to achieve it. This is called your action plan. Then break down the action plan into quarterly, monthly, weekly or daily focused activity. These shorter term action plans keep you accountable to the larger plan and provide legitimate benchmarks on your road to success.

It's a waste of time to set a goal for which there is no realistic action plan. If you are currently earning $5,000 a month and set a goal to earn $100,000 a month inside of twelve months, that's pretty unrealistic. For whatever goal you have, you need the corresponding action plan.

A few years ago, when I started out, I created a goal to earn an additional $3,000-$5,000 a month within a twelve-month period. It was based on the amount of additional sales that I was beginning to work on. It was realistic, based on the additional hours I would be willing to add to my work week and the forecasted future referrals from existing clients. So the goal was to earn this additional income which then required me to work an additional ten hours per week and focus more on asking for referrals. My game plan was then broken down into daily, weekly and monthly scheduled focused activity.

Keep it simple and don't start on too many goals at one time. Accomplishing one very achievable goal in a relatively short amount of time will inspire and motivate you to accomplish others. It's sometimes easy to set big goals and believe they will turn out, when in reality, we can't even begin to understand where to begin. Don't fall for that trap. Start off small and simple and move onto other things. It feels great to meet a goal earlier than you planned and then replacing it with a slightly higher one.

In addition to having a game plan and focused activity, you must develop the ability to visualize the goals occurring in your life. When you start to see something as possible in your life, it becomes a vision. Average people are okay with whatever life gives them. They believe that whatever will happen will happen, so why try for anything else? Wealthy people practice being able to see what they will be doing or what they will have in the future. Your future requires a vision if you are to fulfill your expectations.

A vision operates by the mental images you place in your mind. If I say, "Dog," what do you see? If I say, "Ocean," what do you see? For most people, they don't see the written word "ocean" or "dog." They see a furry, panting, tail-waving animal or a beautiful blue, wavy sea of water. Advertising and marketing firms recognize that people are moved by what they see, and they use visual advertising all the time. They know that if you see something often enough, the chances of you buying it greatly increase.

Getting a vision for something is so much more powerful than having a desire for something. I know a lot of people who are always telling me all the things they desire to do and have in life, but in a couple of months or years, when I see them again, they are not any closer to having them.

Having desire for what you want or even knowing what you want is not enough. Desire and vision are very different:

- A desire is something you want while a vision is something you will have.
- A desire is something you need while a vision is something you cannot live without.
- A desire will give you something to think about while a vision will give you something to live for.
- A desire is something you hope for while a vision is something you get.
- A desire only gives you thoughts of success while a vision brings you to success.

One of the best ways to get a vision produced from your written goals is to take or obtain pictures of them. I like to call it my dream board. I keep one in the bathroom, one on the fridge and one in each of my offices. Throughout the day, as I'm on the phone or grabbing a snack, those pictures are becoming second nature to me. The more I see them, the easier it is to believe they are going to be real in my life.

Like your thinking and belief systems, your life moves in the dominant images you allow yourself to visualize. You and you alone have the power to choose the images that can take you where you want to go.

One of the benefits to having a dream board is the comments you get from individuals who notice the pictures. It provides you with an opportunity to talk about what you are working on. The magic in this is the commitment you are making to accomplish your visually-seen goals. It's a lot harder to back out now that you've just committed to a friend or family member that one day you will achieve that goal.

In addition to your action plan, focused activity and visualization, you need to know the "why" behind what you want. Knowing the "why" behind what you want can be compared to the engine in a car. The goal is the rest of the car, but without the engine tuned to run, you're not likely to go very far. You need to have a big enough "why" to succeed.

We need to have enough compelling reasons to drive us forward to accomplish our goals. Why is becoming a millionaire in the next three years so important to you? It's not about having the greenbacks in the safe-deposit box. It's not because of the money, even though you may believe it is. It's what the money will do for you. Maybe it's the freedom it gives you. Maybe it's the memories you will create with those closest to you by traveling to the places you've always wanted. Or maybe, for someone else, it's the security they will have, knowing that they no longer have to depend on others or their jobs to live well.

That's the "why" or reason behind the goal. When you're tempted to quit and give up, it's the reasons for the goals that will keep you going. Understand your "whys" and be clear about them. I strongly suggest listing them underneath your goals.

We live in a very self-centered and selfish society, and I truly believe the only way to ensure lifelong success is to lead a life full of giving to others and having reasons for building wealth that are so much greater than just you and your immediate family. There is a law of giving and receiving, much like the law of gravity. I can't tell you how it works, but I know for a fact that it does. Give and you shall receive.

A term that has become current in many circles is the Law of Reciprocity. It means that in every relationship, you must give and take mutually and to always return in kind.

> **Knowing the why behind what you want can be compared to the engine of a car.**

It is based on the idea that in every culture on earth, when someone gives something to you, you feel an obligation to give back. It can be either both negative or positive. If you give good to others, they will want to give good back to you. If you harm others, they will seek revenge. In our context, this means that you determine the kind of relationships you will have with people and with the world by how you treat others. If you are selfish, people will tend to be stingy with you. If you are generous, even if it's with attention and compliments or encouragement, it will develop trust in others. Give and you shall receive. It's a principle that works.

There has been much research that documents the fact that the wealthiest people are also the greatest contributors to charities and other great causes. Why would movie stars and people like Bill Gates make the kinds of contributions that they do? Sure, some are only interested in the tax advantages that they get, but it goes much farther than that. Some people call it karma or describe it by saying, "What goes around comes around." It's the fact that they understand the importance of giving to their own well-being.

The best advice I can give on this subject is to encourage you to start now instead of waiting until you have more cash flow. Start by supporting a church or a non-profit corporation that you are passionate about. If you don't start giving now, it will be much more difficult when you are earning a lot more. It's about the habit that you form early on in life. Giving to others and having a life of giving and genuine concern for others around you also creates a strong belief within you that there is more than enough to go around.

For me personally, I am one of the top ten givers in our eight thousand member church. My goal is to be in the top two, not for bragging rights, but because I know what they do with the money is productive and helpful to others in the world. Last year, they supported worldwide missions by giving over one million dollars. It's so much easier for me to give it there because I can trust the integrity and character of this church to do what they say they will do.

Be careful to research wherever you want to give. It's easy for anyone to form a nonprofit organization and say that they have a great cause but then not do the right thing with the money. I know you will agree with me when I say that it's too much effort to earn money and then give it somewhere that doesn't understand integrity.

Wealth is meant to be shared, not hoarded. What a miserable life hoarding is. You can't take it with you anyway, and the average lifespan today is relatively short even at 100 years. The "why" behind your vision for wealth needs to include giving. Some of my personal reasons for building wealth include providing a great life for our parents and family. It's easy once you realize what kind of legacy of giving and sharing you can leave behind.

In today's society, youth and "looking the part" is valued so much that many kids are quick to upgrade their lifestyle and forget about their parents. They quickly make the decision to put their parents in a home so that there is a minimum of disruption in their daily and weekly schedules. It is easy to focus on the mistakes our parents made. But if you're a parent, you'll make some, too. The reality is that we need to get over the past and love our parents with everything we have. Even if they were horrible as parents, they at least brought you into this life and you should be thankful for that, especially now that your life is so great and getting better.

Without getting too personal, my wife and I are going to ensure that both sets of our parents are in store for an amazing rest of their lives. It's not only the right thing to do for them, but it also feels great doing it. It's not our government's responsibility as much as it is yours and mine.

If you take a moment to consider that it probably wasn't easy raising you; there's really a lot to be grateful for. So, make the difference in the lives of your parents and other family members. I believe doing this can be one of the most compelling reasons to build wealth.

Finally, your goals need to include a section where you list your dreams. These are huge goals, things that inspire you and even though you don't know where to get started on them because they are so big, they are still important to have. Dreams can be 5%, 10% or 15% of your goals. Don't worry about putting the action plan together for these yet. Just focus on the short-term ones first. After you've accomplished a couple of these short-term goals, you'll have an idea what it's going to take to accomplish your dreams. Then you can form an action plan for them.

Before reading on, make a list of the things that you want in life and then make the commitment to create your picture dream board over the next two weeks. As you do so, don't forget to list the "whys" for each one.

5

There Will Be Plenty of Time to Sleep When You're Rich

I'm a huge fan of the James Bond movie series. He's such a cool guy. My favorite actor to play Bond is Pierce Brosnan, followed closely by Sean Connery. I think Brosnan was naturally born suave and debonair.

In the movie *Die Another Day*, the bad guy had undergone extensive facial surgery to pretend he was a wealthy British entrepreneur named Graves. James Bond (the Pierce Brosnan version) spent fourteen months in a North Korean prison after his mission is compromised by a betrayal. He is eventually traded for a general's son, the bad guy's brother. Bond sets out on a quest to discover who set him up.

There are some memorable scenes in the film. Among them is one where Graves makes a grand entrance to meet the Queen of England by jumping out of an airplane in a suit. Of course, he lands perfectly as reporters surround him.

One reporter asks him, "Is it true that you never sleep?"

Graves responds with, "You only get one shot at life. Why waste it on sleep?"

In another scene at an ice castle in Ireland, Bond meets with Graves and comments that he looks like a man on the edge. Graves replies, "There's plenty of time to sleep when you're dead."

These statements may be a little extreme. You do need some sleep once in a while but it is extremely important to prioritize your time and make some key decisions about what you do with it. How you manage your time is fundamental to building wealth.

Once you've built the wealth you desire, you will have time to do whatever you want. However, as you begin to build wealth, I suspect that you will not be sleeping very much. That's because there will be so many other fun things to do.

If you were asked, "What is your most valuable asset in life?" How would you respond? Your most valuable asset is not your money. It is your time. I'll prove it to you.

You can always make more money. You can always borrow money. You can work more hours for money. You can work an extra job for money. Well, you get the idea. You can't go and make more time. Once you've spent it, it's gone forever. If you think about the average life span of a person today and consider your age, it puts things in perspective in regard to the value of your time.

I know it's a pretty sobering thought, but I want to drive the point home that time is ticking for every one of us. Average people don't think about how valuable time is. That is why they waste it and think it will never catch up to them. Then one day, they wake up and realize that they could have done some different things with it to create the life they've always dreamed of. I want to encourage you that no matter how old you are, you can get started now with creating what you want by taking control of your time. Everybody starts sometime. It may as well be now.

Time is money. Employers understand this. That's why they want as much effort and production out of every hour for the wage or the salary that they give you. Choose to turn your time into money.

> On average,
> a person wastes
> thirty-five hours
> a week.

I truly believe that the commodity you actually trade for the things you want is the element of time. If you desire a great relationship, you have to invest time into that relationship. If you desire to purchase something, you have to invest time to earn the money to purchase it. If you want to build wealth and leave a legacy for your children, you will have to trade your time to do the right things that will produce that wealth.

On average, a person wastes thirty-five hours a week. I know this sounds crazy but it's true. Let's break it down. There are 168 hours in a week. Forty-five are spent working, which includes commuting. Fifty-six hours are spent sleeping, using the average of eight hours per night. Another thirty-two hours are spent eating, relaxing and spending time with friends and family.

Subtract from the 168 hours ($168 - 45 - 56 - 32 = 35$ hours). Wow, that's thirty-five hours! That's a lot of time. I know some people who don't even work thirty-five hours all week.

Obviously your life is probably a little different than the average. But it would be interesting to find out how these extra thirty-five hours are spent or invested in your own life. If you make a conscious decision to examine where you spend your time, you are now in the position to make some real changes toward building wealth.

In my opinion and based on my personal experience of having done it, I believe anyone can become a millionaire part time in less than three years by using these thirty plus hours a week to do it. Now that we've just found some extra hours in your week, we need to look at how you will be spending that time to build your wealth.

It all starts with doing your "need tos" before your "want tos". This is one of the greatest principles of success that wealthy people live by. Everyone has "want tos" and "need tos" in life. Most of us want to do what we want in life before we do what we need to. We want to have fun, travel and entertain ourselves, but if we don't work or earn money, we won't be able to do these things for very long.

Strengthening your will power and making a life-long decision to do the things you need to do will always insure that you get to do the things you want to do. This is the lifestyle of a wealthy person.

A lot of my wealthy friends and I are driven to work the hours we work, not because we have to anymore, but for two primary reasons. First, it has become a habit and second, it has become a passion. Once you see the progress that you can make, it motivates you even further. It's not about greed for me or just creating additional wealth.

Creating additional wealth is driven by the reasons we discussed in the last chapter. My "whys" motivate me and drive me every day. I hope you had the opportunity to write down and understand yours. It truly will work wonders in your life. When you have clear "whys" and reasons to drive you, it becomes a passion to do the "have tos" before you do the "want tos."

> **Making a life-long decision to do the things you need to do will always ensure that you get to do the things you want to do.**

Let's talk about the keys to managing your time in your business and financial life. I believe the key to effective time management is to develop a realistic and practical schedule. It's all about prioritizing what is most important. What needs to be done first needs to have the first and the greatest amount of attention and the most time allocated to it. Money-making activities are the most important. You can do paperwork or organize anytime, but you only have a certain amount of time to call potential clients or service existing accounts as an example.

Start by taking everything that you know needs to get done and create a complete list. Keep the most important things first and foremost.

After you're done, allocate the things into your weekly schedule in thirty-minute or one-hour increments. Schedule your most important work and the work that requires the most thought in the morning. This will help you focus with fewer interruptions and you'll get more done before your day becomes filled with all the things that normally demand your time.

Decide, if possible, to only take calls during certain times of the day and schedule a time to return phone calls and emails at the same time every day. Phone calls and emails can prove to be a major interruption to scheduled tasks.

Make sure everything is accounted for, and be generous in your time to allow some flexibility through out your day. Try to make sure day-to-day issues don't push your strategic time priorities off your schedule. If you do get off schedule, start back in where you left off.

Work on one thing at a time. Pick one project and if possible, don't move on until it's fully thought through or completed. Every time you work on a project, think of new ways of breaking it down and simplifying it. As you revisit the project the next time, know exactly where you left off by making a note of whatever else needs to be done to complete it.

I have found that maintaining a degree of consistency has helped me to stay focused and get a lot more done. I do the same basic things on Monday, every Monday, that are different from other days in my week. For example, my client follow-ups are primarily done on Fridays and Saturdays. Monday is the day I follow up on all outstanding closings. On Tuesdays, I focus on several other specific assignments. Each day has its primary objectives and work planned with it.

It's effective because it keeps you doing one thing at a time, which helps in getting things done faster. Be realistic and allow time for things that come up and for everyday things such as errands, phone calls, returning messages and emails. When there are interruptions to your week, simply pick up the following week where you left off.

It reduces stress and anxiety to know that all you need to get done every week has been placed in your weekly schedule and will get the time it deserves. Everything has its time and place.

Focus is crucial for time management. The fewer priorities you focus on at once, the more productive you will be. Life will always try to get in the way if you allow it to. It is vital that you maintain focus on your priorities.

In the end, time management is about winning the day. If you focus on winning the day by staying on track with your schedule most of the day, you will win the day. If you do this for the majority of the week, you've won the week. If you win the week more often than not, then you will win the month. And the more months you win, the chances become better that you will win the year. If you win the year, then you probably achieved your goals. But realize that it starts with winning the day. You must focus on the daily planned activity getting done.

The most powerful tool in controlling my time, without a doubt, is the PDA (i.e. Palm Pilot) which is an electronic organizer. By utilizing this technology, my entire schedule is at my fingertips, and I only have to deal with each item once. I think about things and write them down immediately. I set alarms to remind me of things. I set reminders that come up at certain times of the day, week, month or year.

Here are some great ways to get the most out of your PDA. For upcoming meetings or past meetings, I keep the files open and keep them repeating automatically as necessary. By doing this, I keep these meetings fresh and updated.

For calls and other things that need to get done, I create a new section in my calendar that continues to repeat until it's done.

One-time appointments can be set with alarms that go off to remind you about them.

There are either calendar files or memo files for each area of my life that require my attention. I include all areas of my life—personal, business, investment contacts, investment opportunities, my team contact information, all clients' and mentors' birthdays and anniversaries with set alarms and pretty much anything that I may need to think about in the near future.

PDAs have complete phone books and prioritized task lists. Nearly any good one offers memo pads much like Word files in a computer for which you can create specific categories and files.

Unlike a standard paper planner, the magic element a PDA offers is the "find" key. This key is magical. You can type in a word or a portion of a word and it will find all possible matches in your PDA. If you had a meeting with someone and you don't remember their name, you can recall what you spoke about and type in a word that you recall from your notes and all the matches for that word will come up. If you can remember a portion of a phone number, a city or a name, your PDA will do the rest.

You should be able to find a very good one for under $300. Keep in mind how vital it is to continually sync and backup your PDA with your desktop or laptop computer.

As we close out this chapter, let's talk about leveraging your time. I realized years ago that I could save six hours a week if I hired out someone to do my landscaping, pool service, cooking, house cleaning, house maintenance and pest control. There was a time when I couldn't afford the services, but now I can't afford to do them myself.

> **As you become more successful and wealthy, you will want to hire people to do the things that don't make you money.**

I take those six hours every week and invest them into my businesses. As you become more successful and wealthy, you will want to hire people to do the things that don't make you money so that you can focus on doing more of the things that do make you money. You create your future based on how you invest your time. Average people protect their possessions while wealthy people protect their time. Wealthy people understand that protecting their time will create additional possessions.

While we only spoke about your time in relation to your business and earning money, I would encourage you to also create a plan to invest your time with those closest to you. Every week, my family has a family night. The kids decide what we do and nothing gets in the way of that night. Vacations and creating family memories are some of the most important things to me and my family.

We talked about a method for managing time that I use. In the process, make sure you create your own method that works for you. You know your life best. It doesn't have to be exactly like mine or anyone else's. All that matters is that it works for you. Be aware and be in control of how you invest your most valuable asset—your time.

6
LOOKING RICH IS EXPENSIVE

Five years ago, sales in my industry were at an all time low. Quotas were high and commissions had been cut. I had been on a budget intermittently, but I realized I wasn't making enough money. I became discouraged and decided that I would just take things as they became due. I wasn't paying attention to my decreasing income because we were so dependent on credit cards to make ends meet.

It's easy to fall into this situation because it involves making one small decision after another and you lose track of the bigger picture until it just sort of happens. You just go on about your regular life and all of a sudden, you realize that you're spending more than you earn, you're behind on bills and your ship is sinking.

I just kept thinking and telling myself that all I needed was a great month in sales and all my problems would be over. As you can imagine, that month never came, and I was finally faced with the consequences.

I had three jobs at the time. I had the morning paper route from 3:00 am to 6:00 am. I had my regular job from 8:00 am to 5:00 pm. Then I sold Pre-Paid Legal in the evening. It wasn't exactly my dream life, but it was what had to be done.

My family and my wife were supportive, and we made it through. I realize today that having a paper route is hard work, and there are so many other ways to generate more cash flow on a monthly basis.

I don't want anyone reading this book to think that I made great decisions all my life and that I never experienced any struggle outside of my childhood or that when I turned eighteen and I was on my own that I suddenly began to build wealth and everything was great.

I wish that were true, but unfortunately, I had a lot to learn about building wealth. I had the desire to be wealthy, but I didn't have the tools. I know firsthand what it's like to live paycheck to paycheck, charging one credit card to pay another. I know what living at the bottom of the barrel means. I know about bankruptcy and what it's like to do one debt consolidation loan after another. It's not something I'm proud of, but it is something I've been through—and will never go through again. I've learned a lot of what not to do the hard way. I hope that by reading this book, you will use my financial education, rather than tough experience, as your teacher.

When you are in debt and are very short every month, I don't believe that most budgets will work. Like most diets, they take away from people. Any time you take away something from people that requires them to eat less or spend less, it's not something that they are inclined to do for a very long period of time. In a typical budget, people are focused on doing one thing—spending less. And that's not very inspiring.

The spending plan I am presenting, however, focuses first on controlling your expenses and then on the most important part, which is increasing your cash flow. First you need to find out where you are and then you can improve your situation. This plan replaces the focus from spending less to earning more. A person who has controlled his spending and is focused on earning more is going to be a more productive and fulfilled individual compared to the person who is just constantly focused on spending less.

> **In a typical budget, people are focused on doing one thing— spending less. And that's not very inspiring.**

Life all around you is compelling you to spend more, to buy more and generally you can only make your stuff last so long before you have to replace it. It can be an uphill battle when the focus is not on increasing cash flow.

No matter where you are financially or how much money you are making, you need to have a plan for your spending. The more money you make, the more important it is. It's more important because you have so much more money to plan for than when you first got started.

The danger, if you increase your cash flow without first having a spending plan, is that you won't ever realize you are making more because you won't see it. You are too busy spending it to really notice it. Have you ever heard the saying that the more you earn, the more you spend? It's very true unless you've decided in advance where this extra money will go.

The real purpose of your plan is to control what you do with what you have. As I stated earlier, if you are short every month, being concerned with how much less you can spend is not going to provide you with a total solution. Spending less and controlling your expenses is part of the problem, but the majority of the problem is found in not focusing on how to earn more. I've seen a lot of people's budgets. When I sit down with them to discuss their expenses, with the exception of a few monthly bills, they can't usually cut anything else.

So the solution becomes evident. If you can't cut anymore, then you need to increase your income. Since this chapter is primarily about budgeting, we are going to discuss it from the perspective of having a spending plan, but you need to be sure you balance your approach to it. You will then need to find ways to make more. In chapter 9, we will begin to introduce the method and the system whereby you will be able to increase your cash flow, eliminate your debt and start building wealth.

I know a lot of people who don't have a spending plan but who have continued to earn more money and are still living outside of their means. They don't have any real assets to show for it and often just have a bunch of liabilities. They have great cash flow, but they're doing nothing productive with it. Having a spending plan and then adding additional cash flow both work together and are essential to begin the wealth building process.

People today are caught up in the appearance of looking wealthy and not with actually doing what it takes to gain wealth. By leasing or making payments on the high-end consumables, people around them perceive them as affluent when, in reality, they just have a higher cost of living than most people. In addition, because of this, their chances of becoming wealthy are greatly diminished because they have no disposable income left to invest into any great opportunity or to start a business of some kind.

> The truly wealthy aren't concerned with looking wealthy. They are concerned with being wealthy.

People want to live in that nice area and often times do whatever they can to make the purchase, not realizing that their neighbor is there because he has already begun the process of building wealth. The truly wealthy aren't concerned with looking wealthy. They are concerned with being wealthy. They take their disposable income and they invest it in various areas and devote a lot of their attention to building their own business and watching the bottom line. Impressing people is a funny thing because people will pay extra money to drive that nicer car to impress someone they've never met and may not even like if they did meet them.

National research clearly shows that the vast majority of millionaires and wealthy individuals are frugal in their own spending habits. They are not consumed with having to have the latest and greatest, probably because they know they can afford it. They are more consumed with making their money grow in both investments and in their businesses.

I have really nice cars because I enjoy them and because I own them free and clear with the exception of one company-leased vehicle. I don't own them to impress people but because I genuinely love cars and they are a true hobby for me. Besides, the real issue is that I drive my cars for free most of the time and if not for free, then I'm earning money while I drive them. I will share this process in the following chapter; however, the point I'm making here is that it's not about what kind of watch you have, what house you live in, or what car you drive. It's all a matter of personal preference.

Make sure that you are buying these items in a smart fashion — that you can truly afford them and that they are not keeping you from earning more money. Allow the wealth you accumulate to determine and ultimately fund your lifestyle and all the nice things you may want to purchase. Don't let a choice of lifestyle keep you from becoming genuinely wealthy.

Assets and Liabilities

There are two words that I want to make sure you understand—assets and liabilities. Simply put, an asset is something that makes you money and a liability is something that costs you money. A vehicle that you pay $45,000 for out the door and in two years is worth $20,000 is a liability, not to mention the payments you will make in two years' time. It is constantly declining in value.

A refrigerator that you buy for $1,200 that you can only sell for $300 six months later is a liability. I realize that these items are necessities of life, but there are other ways of purchasing them to avoid or drastically reduce the depreciation.

For example, purchase floor models or returned appliances and add a warranty. This will help you extend the life of the item. If you are in a place where you can't afford that item, then don't make $12-a-month payments for fifteen years to buy a fridge. Instead, buy one at a garage sale or by looking in the classifieds.

An asset is something that makes money. Take the same car we just spoke about. I will purchase it when it is six months to a year old from a private owner, thus avoiding the sales tax, doc fees and major depreciation. Now the car is an asset.

Any item that you purchase is neutral. It is how you purchase it and its value after you purchase it that determines whether or not you can call it an asset or a liability. When it's time to purchase something I want or need, I take some extra time and research the good deals and sales coming up. Why would I want to pay more for an item just because I didn't take a few minutes and make a few calls? The money I save on consumables is well into the thousands by the end of the year because we take our time before making the commitment to purchase.

This included remodeling and work around all thirteen of our properties. I obtain at least three bids to determine the best price. I don't always go with the lowest bid. It's more about value than anything. You will always remember value and quality long after you've forgotten the price.

I remember a few years ago, I shopped at a place called Last Chance, which took all the returns from Nordstrom. Sure you had to pay close attention to what you were buying because most of it was used. However, I bought quality slacks that retailed for over $200 for $9.99 and the same with shoes and shirts. I purchased these items less often because the quality was much better than the cheaper brands. It was always interesting seeing the type of people who shopped there. On nearly every occasion I overheard cell phone conversations that tipped me off to the fact that the shoppers were attorneys, doctors or other highly paid professionals.

I don't want to give the impression that we don't impulse buy here and there or that we don't ever buy liabilities. We do. However, my wife and I have made a lifelong decision that our major liabilities will be purchased from the profits or revenues earned from our assets.

For example, for our fifteen year anniversary in 2006, we decided to get the wedding ring she always dreamed of. The ring was five carats and was not cheap. So we invested in a piece of land and some stocks. Then we used the profits from both of those and purchased the ring by writing a single check. By living life this way, we can be assured that we will never return to living outside our means, in spite of the fact that we might purchase some really nice stuff from time to time. It's healthy because we have to take some extra action to get something out of the ordinary or that we've been wanting for some time.

> **You will always remember value and quality long after you've forgotten the price.**

Just a few months ago, we were at the theatre. And I had brought my theatre glass which they sell so you can bring it back in and for a dollar get a refill, which beats $6.50 for a comparable size beverage. We were with a group of friends and one other couple whom I had never met. They were invited by one of our friends. We stood in line to get snacks and he said, "Wow! I'm sorry you had to bring that glass with you. I could have spotted you a few dollars to get the real drink experience."

I kept my cool and said, "Well, maybe next time, I will leave my glass at home and you can buy me a drink."

I laughed and so did a couple of others who knew a little about our financial status. The reality was that I could have purchased all of his liabilities, including his nice home on the lake which he bragged about and still had enough left over to buy a $6.50 drink. What can you say? There will always be ignorant people. Smile and offer to buy them a book and go on with your life because nothing you do will ever change them unless they're ready to make a change. Being frugal is your personal choice. However, actually doing what you read in this book will allow you to spend less because you have an abundance of finances instead of spending less because you have to.

Figuring Net Worth

Before we get started talking about the spending plan, I think it's important to talk about net worth. Net worth is what I like to think of as the most basic and most fundamental way of comparing where you need to be with where you actually are.

Here's an easy way to figure your net worth. Simply multiply your age times your annual total income from all sources and divide that by ten. This is what your net worth should be at your current age. For example, if you're thirty years old and you are earning $38,000 a year, and you have a real estate investment that pays $5,000 a year and another investment that gives you $2,000 a year, you would take the total of $38,000 plus $5,000 plus $2,000, which is $45,000, and multiply that by thirty. This gives you $1,350,000. Divide that by ten and your net worth should be $135,000.

I don't want this to be just another book that you read, enjoy, get a few ideas from and then put on a bookshelf somewhere. I want this to be an interactive experience, something that you decide to actually put into practice and make a part of your life. So let's get started with talking about a great system for a very workable and practical plan for spending.

It starts with identifying all of your expenses in any given month—rent, mortgage, car payments, insurance, utilities, credit card payments, food, gasoline, debt, clothing, entertainment, savings, education and anything else you can think of. Add all of these expenses up for the month and remember to include any other expenses, such as homeowner taxes or anything else that's billed quarterly or yearly. If you realize you have a shortage, we will be sharing how to deal with that in chapter 9, so don't be concerned about it for now. We first have to have a spending plan in place before we talk about increasing cash flow.

The next thing I highly recommend is to set up a checking account and a savings account, if you don't already have one. This checking account is going to be used for your bills. What I mean by bills is your rent or your mortgage, car payments, utilities and anything else that you would typically pay with a check. Try to have auto deposit or direct deposit into this account if possible. This checking account is strictly used for bills. This is not where you get money for shopping for groceries or any other items. This is not the account you eat out with. This money is already set aside for the commitments you have made in the past. Don't take this checkbook or the debit card associated with it anywhere. It should stay at home. You have to make this commitment for your spending plan to work.

The other items that are in your budget, such as groceries, gasoline, clothing, entertainment and related items, should be separated from the bill account. You can do this by withdrawing the total amount of cash or transferring it to an alternate checking account used for this purpose. The reason for doing this is so that you always keep the right amount in the bill account and are never short at the end of the month because you went over on groceries or buying clothes. By separating them, you have ensured that these expenses will not exceed what you've allocated to them.

There are a lot of conflicting methods to determine what percentage of your budget should be allocated to each area. Some people say you should never buy a house that costs double or two and a half times what you earn in a year. That factor, however, in my home state of Arizona, simply doesn't work. Therefore, in an effort to keep things simple and relevant, I want to share only two areas I believe are essential to work into your spending plan. Work them in over time if they are not currently possible.

The first one is savings and investing. I believe you need to be saving 10% of your income toward long-term savings. This 10% is set aside for retirement and not to be used for anything else. For example, mutual funds, 401(k)s, IRAs and CDs.

Don't underestimate how much of a difference long-term savings can make. The following examples illustrate the power of compounding at a conservative rate of return.

Assume, for example, that a person invests with the following:

8% rate of return at $20 per week:
  Ages 18-50, they will have $166,847 in the end.
  Ages 18-30, they will have $22,851 in the end.

8% rate of return at $100 per month:
  Ages 18-50, they will have $193,148 in the end.
  Ages 18-30, they will have $26,536 in the end.

Don't despise small beginnings. If you are consistent, you will have a small start with a big finish.

In addition, I strongly suggest that you build up a three-month reserve account from this 10% for the "what ifs" in life.

The second area I believe very strongly is important, as we discussed previously, is giving. I believe that you should devote at least 10% consistently to this area.

This leaves 80% of your income to live on.

If you don't have these things settled in your life, all you will be doing is getting extra money to increase your lifestyle, but without building wealth. I know a lot of people who make great money and who believe that they do well. They feel great because they have beautiful cars and even nicer homes. They live in the best areas in Phoenix or Scottsdale and life goes on. But they still live paycheck to paycheck because they haven't built a solid foundation of wealth. They've just developed a lifestyle that gives the appearance of wealth.

How much you earn is not as important as what you do with what you keep. What you do with what you keep will decide ultimately if you will be wealthy, and more importantly, if you will stay wealthy. It has been said that making money is easy. Keeping it, however, is difficult. There are a lot of reasons for this statement, and I tend to agree with it. But if you settle in your mind that you're committed to watching the bottom line in living a life of discipline in terms of having your spending plan updated and relevant, your chances of being wealthy and staying wealthy are dramatically increased.

In closing this chapter, I want to add one more comment on giving because I believe it is vitally important to develop that part of your attitude. I was very real and honest about the reasons why I think this is so important and ultimately, the choice is yours, but I hope you will agree with me and feel compelled to do it. You can make money without giving, but I believe that part of holding on to wealth is learning how to use it for the good of those around you, not just for your own gratification.

It is my personal conviction that the focus of your giving should be a local church and at the risk of appearing to impose my own spiritual convictions, I want to encourage you to consider your own involvement. If you are not already in a church, I believe it would be of great benefit to you in every area of your life, including your finances, to find one that you can be a part of. Find one that is active in the community and gives to causes that affect the world such as missions. In some ways, the church can make it easier for you to discern whether or not an organization is appropriate for your gifts.

My wife recently became interested in giving to a cause in Cambodia. Rather than devoting a great deal of time and energy to verifying the organization to ensure that the money would actually go where it needed to, I simply spoke to my church accounting department and shared with them my desire. Their resources for researching the organization were much better than mine anyway.

Now we periodically designate a portion of our church offerings to that cause. They take care of the rest. I get a tax deductible receipt or statement at the end of the year, and life is easy.

> How much you earn is not as important as what you do with what you keep.

In addition to this, our church supports numerous other organizations and missions worldwide. I would never be able to keep up with writing those checks every month. It's much more practical to put the money in their hands, knowing it will have worldwide impact.

A second reason for my suggestion that you find a great church is because a lot of the success I've experienced has been a direct result of the practical messages I've heard there. Most churches today recognize that they need to provide practical and relevant information that helps people live a great life. No matter what kind of a terrible week I may have had or what challenges I might be going through, I know I can show up on Sunday and be accepted, supported and challenged. The church I belong to even began a business college which has been instrumental in both starting new businesses and growing existing ones.

In closing, before reading on, take a few minutes and create your spending plan. It will form the platform from which you can begin building wealth.

7

WORKING FOR MONEY IS HARD WORK

W orking for money really is hard work. Working for yourself and working for your goals, working for your family and working for what really matters to you comes pretty easily. In America today, and certainly in other parts of the world, most people work for a paycheck which they need to survive. It's pretty sad when you think about it, especially in America. We live in a land of opportunity. People from all over the world immigrate here to have a fighting chance of success. They literally risk their lives in exchange for an opportunity to live in America.

It has been estimated that on average, if someone misses his paycheck for more than five weeks, he will go bankrupt and would have no other way of living or surviving. In this chapter, we're going to provide you with a goal of having money work for you so that you don't have to work for it anymore. I realize that if this is the first time you're hearing this, it may sound a bit unachievable or unattainable. But in reality, it's not that difficult.

When you have money working for you, it doesn't matter if you get laid off or if you lose your job. It doesn't really matter what happens in the economy. When you have money working for you, very few things can ever affect your life and determine your ultimate success. It's really a simple process when you have money working for you. It's not rocket science. It's very simply a matter of having your assets outweigh your living expenses. When the money that you're earning from your investments and your businesses are in excess of what it costs you to live, then money is working for you.

Before starting this chapter, you should have identified and executed a realistic and attainable spending plan for your life. You can't begin to have money work for you if all you do is continue to spend everything you earn.

The world economic system doesn't want you to have money work for you. It wants you to continue to be dependent on it. The world system needs employees. Companies need employees, but the real issue is: do you want to be an employee and work for money the rest of your life? That's why life can sometimes seem like it's a trap. Everyone is offering you free credit. Make the minimum payment, finance for ten years. It all seems so appealing and so easy. You get into a life and a lifestyle full of debt, full of purchasing and owning liabilities. There's little or no money left over to invest. You get yourself into a situation where you're working seventy or eighty hours a week and spending more than you earn. I like to call this the rat race. The world system lives to keep you in it.

The only way to break this vicious cycle is to increase cash flow into your life, not to spend it, not to buy nicer things and more liabilities, but to put it into business and other investments. Every one of us, for the most part, starts off as an employee, but we don't have to stay there.

We're going to get to the practical ways of how to increase your cash flow and build wealth, but before we get there, we have to become educated. I'm not talking about a college degree, even though that's great. I don't mean education the way most people think of it. I'm talking about financial education and becoming financially literate.

So what is financial literacy? I believe that if I were to sum it up in one sentence, it would be knowing how money actually works in the real world. I can tell you that most people never study the subject of financial literacy. Our public school systems don't teach it. Colleges don't teach it. Business colleges don't teach it and most seminars and late-night infomercials don't teach it, either.

> The rich continue to become richer because they understand what it means to invest their money.

Public schools and colleges and the education system provide you with an education. But having a financial education or being financially literate means understanding money and the way it really works and why the rich get richer and the middle class and the poor seem to get poorer. The rich continue to become richer because they understand what it means to invest their money and continue to not only make their investment back but also to profit. Middle class and poor people continue to upgrade their lifestyle and invest in liabilities.

I have family members and friends who earn great money and every time they get a raise, it's all about buying that new toy, that new car or taking that dream vacation. Every time I get a raise or I make a little extra money, it has been about where I can put it to make even more money. I want my money to make money for me.

Do you see the contrast here? That's why the rich keep getting richer. They understand investments and they love to profit. From the profit, they buy their liabilities. A huge key to true wealth is delayed gratification, realizing that you can't have everything that you ever wanted today. I believe it is healthy and will help you stay focused on building wealth.

Wealthy people understand assets and liabilities. We talked a little bit about them in the last chapter but we're going to take it to another level here. Average people buy liabilities, not because they want to be broke but because they are striving to do well and just don't know what other way to do it. They truly do believe their liabilities are assets and they do not have the financial education or literacy to realize that the things they have purchased are not in fact assets. Be careful who you allow to give you financial advice—bankers, real estate agents, financial planners, insurance agents or anybody else who thinks he knows something about money and wants to teach you something. You need to consider the results they have in their own lives first. They need to understand assets and liabilities and be financially educated. Some financial planners may themselves not have any kind of financial literacy. They may only be self-employed, looking after their own commissions. Different licensed professionals talk negatively about other investments in order to push their product.

Let's take a deeper look into assets and liabilities. Once you have financial education, you can tell them apart with no problem at all. You need to be able to follow an asset all the way through taxes and other related expenses to see if it really is an asset and know if it really does make you money.

One of the biggest items that people believe is an asset is really a huge liability—their cars. People brag, "I got a low interest rate and I'm getting a great deal and making an investment into my future by buying the car I've always wanted." They buy the car for $45,000. They make payments for five years. At the end of the five years, the car that they bought for $45,000 plus the interest over that time is now worth $10,000 if they're lucky. The car now has almost 100,000 miles and is approaching being out of warranty.

The next thing most people do is decide they want to invest in the future some more. They could easily sell the car for $10,000 but instead they trade the car in. The dealer gives them $2,500 and says it's a great deal and they start all over again. If you follow it all the way through, that is not an asset. It's a liability.

I have a great system for buying cars and having them be assets most of the time. When they are not assets, they are an even tie with a liability. Sometimes it's right in the middle. They don't cost me any money, but they also didn't make me any money. Even if I don't make money on a car that I own, I think that's still a great deal considering I got to drive it for free. I've been doing this since I was about twenty-one years old.

Back in those days, I didn't have a whole lot of money to work with and so what I would do is find a vehicle that I could afford somewhere between $2,000 and $3,000. I would buy the car for cash. I would clean it up and do any minor repairs that it needed and I would immediately place an ad in the classifieds for it. I would drive the car typically a month to three months before it would sell. I wouldn't lower the price too much because, after all, it was a car I was driving and, in some cases, I wasn't really too motivated to sell it. Not being motivated to sell it caused me to get what I wanted for the cars most of the time.

I had a system that I stuck with that really worked and I still use it today. First of all, I would never buy a vehicle with over 80,000 miles. The reason for that is most cars are beginning to develop major problems or have problems that are occurring at that point which is why people are selling them in the first place. In addition, most people are not looking for a car with these miles because their perception is that it's not going to run for very much longer. I'm not a mechanic and I can't verify which cars last longer than others. The issue was people's perceptions that led them to make decisions either to buy or not buy vehicles with a certain number of miles.

In addition, I would research, based on what the cars were actually selling for in publications like the Auto Trader and the local newspaper. It didn't matter and it still doesn't matter what Kelley Blue Book or other services similar to it say the car should be worth. All that really matters is what people are selling the car for. Once I find the make and model that seems to be holding its value and for which there seems to be just a few of them available for sale, I target that type of car. I don't buy makes and models of which there are substantial amounts available for sale. I don't want to have a lot of competition drive the price of the vehicle down.

> **I had a system that I stuck with that really worked and I stilll use it today.**

The second thing I would do is to verify if the miles are original. Back in those days they didn't have such convenient sources as they do today. I love CARFAX. So what I had to do and I still do today, in addition to CARFAX, is I would ask them a series of questions before I saw the car such as how long they've owned it and why they are selling it. The biggest question that led me to what I was looking for was always my last question, tossed out as though I didn't care too much and it wasn't that big of a deal. But it was a major issue that I needed to know. The question was, "Who did you buy it from?" I would later verify this question by looking on the title or by looking at it in the bill of sale that they provided so they knew they couldn't lie and not be found out before the transaction was over.

This question, if it provoked anger, which it did most of the time, was due to the fact that the individual had purchased the car in an auction or was a dealer in disguise. For whatever reason, people like to sugarcoat or flat out lie about the fact that they own a car with a salvaged title or something less than normal on the title. If this was the case, I wouldn't touch it with a ten foot pole.

No matter what kind of a great deal you might think you're getting, most banks won't finance such cars and most prospective buyers don't want anything to do with them either. Individuals locate these vehicles from insurance companies and body shops and buy them for pennies on the dollar. Who knows the workmanship that went into them to repair them? They get them back to their original condition so that they can turn around and sell them for high profits.

In such cases, I was not interested. My system, then and now, means I only buy from private owners who have owned the vehicle for a minimum of a year. I don't do this because I have a phobia of dealers or auctions but because people's perception, much like with high mileage, is that they don't want an auction car or a vehicle that showed a series of dealers owning it. I quickly learned this and only purchased first- or second-owner vehicles. When I resold them, I advertised it in big, bold letters. People, for whatever reason, feel like if it's a first or second or third owner vehicle, it's a good car. For the most part I have to agree.

The third thing I would do is take the car to a mechanic. As I mentioned, I wasn't very mechanically inclined so I needed to depend on someone whom I could trust to look over the vehicle and insure that there were no major problems with it, since I planned to sell it. I also had a mechanic, to the best of his knowledge, try to verify if the miles seemed original by looking at the number of parts under the hood that were original or recently replaced.

My mechanic would always legitimately find something wrong with the vehicle, minor or major. I would then assess what it was going to cost me to get that item fixed with him and I would use that as a point of negotiation with the owner. Typically the owner was present and could find out for himself what was wrong with the vehicle he was trying to sell me. If he knew it already, he seemed upset and defensive and if he didn't realize it beforehand, he would be apologetic and gladly negotiate the difference.

Depending on what was wrong with the vehicle and after I made the purchase, I would either fix it or, in some cases, just tell the prospective buyer about the problem in advance. As long as I was asking a fair price and was being honest about what I knew, they didn't have a problem with it.

Today my price range is a little bit different so I only buy vehicles that carry the original manufacturer's warranty and that have less than 20,000 miles. I don't take the cars to mechanics anymore. I simply get the VIN number and call the dealer to verify the warranty on the vehicle and the last services that were done on it. A dealer typically has access to some service that's overdue or coming up and I always use that as a negotiating tool and it works 80% of the time. If you can afford to buy vehicles in this price range that carry an original manufacturer's warranty, you eliminate all the risk of buying a car that has potential major problems.

However, do not forget to verify with the dealer the current status of the warranty. I've had the experience before of a vehicle owner telling me that the warranty on the car expires in a certain month and year, only to find out from the dealer that the warranty was not nearly as long as the owner thought. The reason for this is that the manufacturer's warranty starts from the date of in-service or the month it was created and shipped.

I highly recommend using CARFAX anytime before you buy a vehicle. It's not 100% accurate, but it does offer some strong guarantees. They guarantee that the vehicle was never in an accident, that the mileage is original and that the title is clean.

Whether you finance the vehicle or you pay cash is really up to you. The bottom line is that you're are buying a vehicle for a certain price, then driving it for a few months and, in most cases, selling it for more than you paid for it.

Finally, be aware of your state's Department of Motor Vehicles rules and regulations before buying too many cars within the same year.

If you thought your car was an asset, but now see it as a liability, how do you view your house? Some people believe that houses are liabilities because they cost you money. They cost money on upkeep and interest in mortgage payments and insurance and in general repairs, so it has to be a liability. Right?

I disagree. It depends on whether the house is worth more than you owe on it. In Arizona, where I live, I am actively involved in real estate investing. I consider my own personal home to be an asset. Sure, it costs me a lot of money every month for maintenance and upkeep but the reality is that it has gone up $200,000 in the last twenty-four months. The increase in value means that it is making more money for me. I call that an asset. If I needed to pull out a second mortgage, or if I needed to sell the home, I have access to that money, and if I play my cards right and keep my personal home over two years, I can avoid all of my taxes.

> Having a spending plan and being able to control your expenses are part of being financially literate.

I realize that in some areas, homes may not be an asset. In order to find out whether your home or anything else you own is an asset or a liability, you have to be able to follow through the numbers and look at everything realistically and be able to answer the question, "Am I making money or am I losing money?" Not understanding where you are financially, not understanding how much money you need to make a month, not knowing how much debt you owe, are all part of being financially illiterate. Having a spending plan and being able to control your expenses are part of being financially literate.

People place a great value on having a college degree or an education, when in reality, that may guarantee them a great income as an employee, but it does not guarantee that they will ever build wealth. My wife and I are teaching our children financial literacy at an early age and giving them a great financial education. My daughter, who is nine years old, understands the difference between a liability and an asset. I mean that she can really tell you what it means. And practically, she thinks about it and she spends her allowance and is using it to earn money. She realizes, even at her age, that once she spends a dollar, she'll never see it again. She's beginning to realize her greatest assets are her mind, her ideas, her time and her ability to solve problems.

I personally only started college and never finished. I could tell you that it was because of financial reasons that I had to drop out in order to work and earn money. But that really is only an excuse. I frankly just did not enjoy going to school. That's the truth. I thought for years after I stopped going to college that it was the biggest mistake I ever made. I regretted it deeply and someday planned on returning and getting my degree.

However, the more my financial education from reading books, attending seminars and listening to CDs increased, the more my wealth began to grow and the more I realized that having a college degree was not able to provide me with this sort of education. Times were different back in the 30's, 40's and 50's. You could go get a college education and a great job. You could make a career out of it and then you could look forward to a comfortable pension and retirement.

Today, it's just not that way. That's why I place an emphasis on a financial education in addition to a college degree. I'm not saying that you need one or the other. What I am saying is that the financial education will take your college education to the next level. Our world needs doctors, teachers and engineers, so I'm not saying we all need to avoid college and exclusively learn to invest to become wealthy. You can do both as long as you are committed to building wealth and doing what you enjoy doing.

Four Different Income Streams

There are four types of income that you can potentially earn. The first is from being an employee. The second is from being a self-employed individual. The third is from being a business owner and the revenues that owning a business would generate. The fourth is from being an investor, generating income from investments of all kinds.

The categories are self explanatory. You obviously know which category you fit into at the moment by the type of income that you receive. However, the reason for sharing this is to bring to your attention not only which category you are in, but to get you to think about which category you should be in. The goal is to try and get you from being an employee or even a self-employed person to that of a business owner and an investor.

Doctors, lawyers, and realtors are self-employed, but if they don't go to work that week or that month, they typically wouldn't get paid. Unless they have a system in place that allows them to continue earning money without having to do much work in exchange for it, they have to show up and perform some task.

I'm not knocking people who are self-employed. I'm just stating the reality. If you ask most self-employed people, they would admit that they are married to their business, and if they don't show up for work, they don't get paid. I do believe, however, that as a self-employed person, it's easier to transition to being a business owner.

Having a business means owning a system that produces income regardless of whether or not you show up for work. A self-employed person probably already has some sort of service or product that he needs to create a system for, a system that would eliminate him from having to personally do what it takes to produce the income. However, becoming a business owner and realizing income from a business without having to continually show up is going to require not only having a system in place, but it will require leadership skills as well. Leadership skills are vital in a business because you need to create a team of people who work for you.

Becoming an investor is not just about saying that you own an investment. It's about whether or not that investment is actually making you money. People who say that they are professional investors typically are professionals who are self-employed but not actually investors. The reason for this is that they have to show up for work in order to get paid anything. They still have to do something. The money is not working for them. They are still working for the money.

An employee works for money. A self-employed person also works for money, even though he owns his job. A business owner owns a system and has people work for him.

An investor has money working for him. The goal is to become an investor and a business owner and have money begin to work for you instead of you having to work for it. It's not something that can happen overnight. It's a progression and it takes some time, some commitment and a little skill. But ultimately, this is where you want to be—either owning your own business system or investing or both.

> **Leadership skills are vital in a business because you need to create a team of people who work for you.**

Just because you read this book and begin to earn some money doesn't necessarily mean that you have money working for you. The real question is, if you don't do the work or if you don't show up for work, will you still get paid? At the time of writing this book, I am self-employed. I'm one-third partner in eight different businesses and I am building my investor income. My goal is, within five years, to make the transition from business owner to 100% investor. I still plan to be self-employed because I thoroughly enjoy what I do. As I begin to do this, I will simply hire somebody to run all of my businesses, which probably by that time will be somewhere around twenty.

So where do you fit in? Are you an employee, self-employed, have a business or have an investment income? In chapter nine, we will discuss my system to change where you are now to where you want to be.

Taxes

One of the reasons why the rich continue to become richer is that they pay less in taxes compared to average people. It's been estimated that paying taxes is a person's highest expense in life. I totally agree.

As an employee you quickly realize how many deductions are withdrawn from your check and how it affects your take home pay. I remember, at fifteen years old, getting my first paycheck at Whataburger. I had worked thirty-three hours that week and I thought I was going to be a millionaire. Then I saw my check and I asked, "When do I get the rest of my money?" I wasn't financially intelligent at the time but I could multiply thirty-three hours times $4.75 an hour.

Average people who aren't financially literate are looking for the best deal at the end of the year for someone to prepare their personal tax returns. Or they prepare their own returns. If I had something wrong with my leg and needed surgery, I would never perform surgery on myself unless I was on a deserted island. People who go to a tax preparer who just works once in a while to make a quick $50 get exactly what they pay for.

Wealthy people hire the best and the most proficient and experienced individuals to not only prepare their taxes but also to advise them how to avoid taxes (legally) or pay the minimum required. You would think it would stand to reason that rich people have to pay more in taxes because they earn so much more money. But the reality is that, while they do earn more, they also pay much less. I'm not saying that we all need to figure out ways to avoid taxes. My point here is that we need to be financially educated and literate enough to know what we are required to pay and not give up a dime more. I like to know when I'm giving my money away. I don't want to give money away when I'm not aware of it.

The cost of cheap advice is too expensive. Years ago, I was using someone to complete and file my returns who charged me under $125.00. I was more concerned with the price of the service than her experience and expertise. I was referred to someone different and began to use her as my accountant. From one year to the next, without any considerable changes in income and write-off's I received a substantially larger tax return. A person's qualifications and experience really do matter and can have an impact on your results.

So how do the rich people pay fewer taxes? They do it by learning tax loopholes—legal ones. They also do it by forming companies and corporations which provide a great deal of tax benefits.

People who are self-employed and believe that a sole proprietorship is the same as owning their own company are making a big mistake. A sole proprietorship is taxed the same way an individual is. For starters, sole proprietorships, like the self-employed, pay self-employment taxes where a company does not. So, for example, if a person with a sole proprietorship earns $100,000 in a year, he might pay a higher amount in taxes, even after all the great write-offs that he was able to include.

Based on the same amount of income, compare a sole proprietorship to a Corporation. While they both make the same amount of money, $100,000, a corporation is allowed to deduct expenses which are taken from the amount of income earned. As a result, the amount of taxes this company pays should be substantially less.

Besides some other tax benefits, the biggest key is the difference between a write-off and an expense. The problem with write-offs is that you already paid for it once. For example, if you write off mileage, you are using after-tax dollars to pay for the gas and then at the end of the year, using the write off method, you are only getting a fraction of credit towards your tax liability.

Contrasted with an expense of a company or corporation, the same mileage issue is treated totally differently. The company car is fueled with money provided by the company. This is an expense that is directly deducted from income that the company earns. If the company earned $1,000 a month and accumulated $300 in gasoline expenses that month, they are only going to be taxed on the remaining $700, not the original $1,000. In addition, now the company may also qualify for credit in the way of depreciation on the actual vehicle that it owns at the end of the year. This depreciation may even be greater if the vehicle is leased. There's so much that needs to be said about the benefits of a company compared to an individual. I highly recommend reading a book entitled *Own Your Own Corporation* by Garrett Sutton, Robert T. Kiyosaki and Ann Blackman. It is one of the *Rich Dad's Advisor Series* and is absolutely excellent. It will not only educate you concerning the tax benefits, but also explain how to protect your assets. It will give you everything you need to form your own companies.

So, to begin with, make it a personal goal to find and hire the best accountant that money can buy. I don't care if you were paying $100 a year for your tax return to be done and now you're paying $1,000. I can assure you that this is money well spent. By paying for a better accountant, someone who is more qualified and experienced and who understands tax law and the benefits that you're entitled to, you can save anywhere from two to five times the amount you just paid for their services. In addition, make sure that they are well-versed in corporate tax returns. If possible, try to find a CPA who is also a tax strategist. Unless you have a good referral and know about their proven track record, I would interview three and pick the best one. Once you make your decision, make it a point to discuss with them whether or not you're eligible to or how you can go about benefiting from forming a corporation.

> **Make it a personal goal to find and hire the best accountant that money can buy.**

Good Debt and Bad Debt

There's a big buzz going on in society that says "Get out of debt and stay out of debt." I certainly agree with getting out of debt, but I want to take this opportunity and point out the difference between bad debt and good debt. Just because something has debt associated with it does not mean that it's all bad. It's great if somebody gets out of debt and does not owe any more money, but without financial education and literacy, it will be only a matter of time before they end up in the same situation. If they don't know the difference between an asset and a liability, as I stated before, they continue to buy items that they think are assets when, in fact, they are total liabilities.

Bad debt is debt associated with liabilities. Credit cards that were used to buy non-appreciating items as well as other department store charge accounts can all be considered as bad debt.

A few years ago, my wife and I made a decision that if we couldn't afford it by writing a check, we wouldn't buy it. It was as simple as that. It was a tough decision at first because we were so used to consumer debt. It was so easy to make an application, to get approved and to go on about life with the $18-a-month payment. We never felt the pain of an $18-a-month payment, but by the same token, we never considered we weren't paying toward the debt. Most of our payment was going toward interest.

Finance companies and banks love people who live this way. I think it's a love/hate relationship because the moment you're late, they're not very loving anymore. They have no sympathy and no mercy because you have fourteen other accounts just like them and are having problems with paying each of them. They're not the ones that made a bad decision, however. You are. You are responsible for your own decisions, for the purchases, good and bad.

So what is good debt? Good debt, as you can imagine at this point, is debt on assets or things that are making you money. For example, if I see a home that's worth $200,000 that's being sold for $120,000 but I can't pay for it with cash, I am going to borrow the money to buy it because it's an asset and a money-making investment. I'll buy the home. I'll do whatever needs to be done to it and turn around and sell it. It doesn't matter what I end up doing with the home. I will most likely see a profit by going into this good debt situation. I will make a lot more money than the interest will cost me.

Of course, you've got to take into account taxes, real estate fees and other expenses, but you see the point I'm making. I am very excited to borrow money at 7% interest when I can earn 18%. My profit is still 11% and yes, I had to use some debt to do it. But that debt ended up making me money.

It's the same with vehicles. Depending on the number of vehicles that I own at the time and where my other money is invested, I will sometimes buy the car for cash and turn around and get a loan on it. Because I bought the vehicle outright to begin with, it doesn't bother me to have a loan on it. For example, I purchased my second H2 Hummer SUV last year for $44,000. I used cash to negotiate the best price so that the buyer didn't think I needed to have a loan which I didn't need but had planned on getting because of an upcoming investment I would need it for. Sometimes buyers are patient but other times, if you have cash, you can greatly increase your chances of getting a much better price.

So I did my negotiations. The vehicle was originally priced for $52,000 and over a period of a couple of days, we ended up at $44,000. The day after I bought the H2, I went to my bank and borrowed the maximum loan amount of $48,000. I reimbursed my investment account $44,000 and I place the other $4,000 in the stock market. Ten months later, I sold my Hummer for $45,500 to purchase a newer one with less miles. Because I had been making payments on my car loan, my payoff was $45,670. The person who bought the vehicle from me needed a loan and his bank paid off my loan along with a personal check from me for $170 to make up the difference in the payoff.

From the time I had purchased the vehicle until the time I sold it, I had made $1,500. In addition, the $4,000 dollars I had borrowed from the bank above and beyond the original cost of $44,000 was still in the stock market and had made me an additional $2,350. So the bottom line was that in ten months, by using good debt, I had made $3,850. Because I financed the vehicle instead of using my own money of $44,000, I made an additional $6,100 in profits. If you combined the $6,100 with the $3,850, I made $9,950 by using good debt. The only real cost to me for owning the vehicle was the monthly payments that I was making for ten months. But that's pretty standard. You typically will have the monthly payment of some kind, except that mine was working for me by paying off the principal balance and making me this additional $9,950. I love to borrow money because I know I can turn around, pay the money back and still make a profit. There are so many ways to do this besides vehicles and real estate that the possibilities are endless.

Unless you have a plan and a strategy, however, for making money by borrowing money, you probably shouldn't borrow it. Stick with having no debt at all and work up to investing at a reasonable level.

Not Increasing Your Lifestyle and Getting Comfortable

One of the biggest dangers that you will ever encounter will be that once you begin to see this extra money come in, you will be tempted to think of all the great things that you can do with it. You're going to have pressure from your spouse, family, kids, friends and coworkers. They're all going to tell you what you need to do with this extra money. You need to relax. You need to take it easy. Play more golf or whatever. They're going to tell you how badly you need a great vacation and then they're going to tell you where you need to go to take it, not because they've been but because they read it in a magazine somewhere.

I've fallen into this trap. Not so long ago, I started to believe that I had worked hard, that I had earned something great and that I was onto something good and therefore it was time to take it easy. I started to work fewer hours every week. I started to focus more on entertainment and recreation and less on my business and investing. "After all," I thought, "I've put enough time into them and now they will continue to grow without me."

My goals were still out there, waiting for me to catch up to them, but I allowed everyone around me, including myself, to stop and relax. I'm not saying you can't take a break every once in a while. I'm not saying you can't take a vacation and I'm not saying that you can't buy nice stuff along the way. But if you stop long enough, you may never get started again. Life can just become too comfortable at times. That's why having compelling reasons and under-standing your reasons behind building wealth is so vital to your success. They not only keep you going when you're discouraged but they'll keep you going when you get com-fortable and satisfied, too.

Aboard a cruise ship on the Mexican Riviera, I was talking with my mentor, Tom Anderson, and I began to de-scribe to him how great life was, how easy I was taking it and how I felt that I had accomplished something great. But then I began to tell him that I was starting to feel increas-ingly more dissatisfied as the weeks went on. He already knew what I was going through before I even told him. He had experienced and continues to experience great success in investing in real estate, as well as other forms of invest-ment. Needless to say, he was doing quite well and was a lot better off than me. I didn't care, though. It was time for me to stop and relax and enjoy life.

I can't tell you exactly what he told me or how he told me but in a matter of a two-hour conversation, I real-ized how stupid it was for me to stop and enjoy life. I real-ized that I would enjoy life a lot more as I was moving to accomplish my goals. I went back to my state room that afternoon and I did some soul-searching and realized how close I had come to sinking back into mediocrity.

I decided right then and there that the next time I wanted to take a break, I would remember the reasons I had for building wealth and allow them to motivate me and inspire me. It was just the very beginning. I moved on and made the necessary adjustments and today, only a year and a half later, I am miles ahead of where I ever dreamed I could be from the day I had that conversation with Tom Anderson.

> **Life can just become too comfortable at times.**

I share this story because I believe it is relevant and may at some point occur in your life. Make the choice to make a commitment to continue moving forward to have money work for you. In doing that, you will find relaxation and enjoyment. Having money work for you is fun. Working for money is hard work. When you're tempted to stop and enjoy life, reevaluate your goals. Make them bigger than yourself and allow them to drive you to future success.

We talked about a lot of different things in this chapter and I want to take a moment to summarize. Learning to have money work for you is something you'll do for the rest of your life. The more I study, the more I realize all the things I don't know. The more I realize all the things I don't know, the more I realize I want to know. Your mind is your most important investment. Make a commitment to learn more about money, ways to make more of it, ways to invest it and ways to keep more of it. You tend to become what you study. It affects your thoughts. Then it affects your belief system, which ultimately affects your decision-making process.

8

PURPOSE DRIVEN WEALTH

Being born and raised in El Paso, I always knew there was one name that goes hand in hand with the city. That name is Chico's. The fast food restaurant, Chico's Tacos, was established in 1953 and soon became known as the best and most famous restaurant not only in the city, but across the region. In fact, *The El Paso Times* recently had an article on the top reasons why people visited El Paso. You guessed it. The number one reason why people visit is to eat at Chico's Tacos.

All I can tell you is that you either really love it or you really hate it. There are very few people who are neutral. Some of the cheapest and lowest grade ingredients go into making these amazing tacos. They're tightly rolled and then deep-fried and placed in a red-checkered, cheap cardboard, rectangular container. They serve the tacos buried in a red tomato-based hot sauce topped with grated cheese.

I think the life expectancy of the container is under an hour. After that, it begins to lose its form and will begin to leak. That's okay, because people generally devour them within five minutes. I know they don't sound very inviting the way I've described them, but if you were there and could taste them, there's a good chance you would love them. If not, then you would hate them. You wouldn't be ambivalent.

Don't bring a credit card or a checkbook. They only take cash and maybe a peso or two, but the good news is that you can feed a family of four for under $12.00. Most of the employees speak only Spanish, and because I'm bilingual I enjoy watching people who don't speak Spanish when ordering their food.

I've taken a lot of my friends over the years to Chico's and some of them tell me they can't even handle the smell inside the restaurant. They find it completely repulsive. Of course, I don't smell it because I'm addicted to the tacos. However, you might be well advised to use the restroom before going to Chico's. That's just my opinion.

To give you an idea of the level of my addiction, I spoke to the owners on several occasions about opening a franchise. I lived eight hours away, after all. They smugly said, "No, thank you."

So I purchased an expensive freezer which I keep in my garage and I purchased six months worth of these tacos. There is a whole system that I created to keep everything separate, and I bought the most expensive containers money could buy. For me, money is not an object when it comes to wanting some of these tacos.

Needless to say, everyone at some point has tried to reproduce and remake these amazing taco wonders. No one has ever been successful but everybody still keeps trying. Some say it's the cheese and others say it's the sauce. No one really knows. Regardless of which is true and despite how cheap the ingredients are, there are lines of people waiting to buy tacos from 10:00 am to 3:00 am at every Chico's Tacos in town.

Similar to the magical recipe of Chico's Tacos, I believe that there are necessary ingredients that will cause you to build wealth for a lifetime. I like to call using these ingredients purpose-driven wealth. Building wealth will require you to purpose doing what works. Purpose in your life to do the following things to build wealth and enjoy a great life in every area.

These are general principles that apply to all forms of relationships, businesses, investments as well as your career.

Purpose to Be a Problem Solver

Having a high IQ is great but having the increasing ability to solve problems will not only get you promotions, but also produces success in business and investments. A high IQ means you are smart and highly intelligent. However, I know a lot of highly intelligent people who do not know how to solve problems in life. Being a problem solver means you have a higher capacity to see through the problem right to the solution. Having a high IQ makes it easier to solve problems, but it is certainly not a requirement.

Promotions and raises always go to the problem solvers in life because their company needs someone who can think about solutions and increase the bottom line with their implementations. A person is paid based on what kinds of problems they solve. A person who solves the problem of maintaining your lawn is paid a certain amount while another person solves the problem of performing surgery and is paid quite a different amount. The issue is what problems you choose to solve and are trained to solve. Think about what problems your company or your own business is facing and how to solve them.

Being a problem solver is a prerequisite to building wealth because society rewards people who solve problems. The person who invents a much needed item is paid very well for doing so. At the very foundation of running a business is being able to solve a problem for your customers. When a business ceases to solve problems, customers stop coming and the company goes out of business. Think about what problems need to be solved, then solve them and you will have developed a great, innovative business idea. Before solving a problem, be very clear about who will benefit from such a solution. Who are you solving it for? That's so that you ensure that you are solving it for the right kind of customer and that the market is viable.

Investing money is solving a problem for someone or something. When you invest in real estate, for example, you are solving the problem that people have for shelter. Investing in real estate pays a different amount than solving the problem for a bank needing your money to reinvest. Investing in tax liens solves the problem that the county has of getting past due tax bills paid immediately. In turn, the county ensures that the taxpayer who is in arrears pays you back with a decent rate of return on your money during a specific period of time. If they do not pay, the county insures that the property will pass on to you, sometimes for just the cost of the original tax lien you already paid. Because the investing rule of thumb is the greater the risk, the greater the return, the key to investing smarter is determining which investment has diminishing risk and maximum return.

A problem solver, while being aware of the problems, looks past them and comes up with any and all potential solutions to them. Solving problems is not difficult. It just takes determination and a little time. Look for the problems that need to be solved so that you can get paid. Average people complain about the problems and spend all their time asking others to solve them.

> **Look for the problems that need to be solved so that you can get paid.**

Realizing how little time families have today to prepare meals and how expensive it is to eat out, we started looking at solutions. At the time of this writing, this is a problem we are in the process of solving by purchasing an already existing food preparation company. This company prepares the types of meals that families order and makes them available to pick up once a week. They can be stored and then simply warmed up for a fresh, healthy meal.

Consider the new areas where you live that are being developed and may not have the availability of shopping necessities in the area of dining, entertainment and services like dry cleaners. People in these areas have a problem for which you may be able to provide a solution. What is something that a lot of people today have very little of?

There may be many things but a key shortage is time. People want more time for themselves, their families and for entertainment. That's a problem and will require new and innovative solutions on many levels. Be a part of solving the problem so that you will be rewarded financially.

Purpose to Build Your Team

In life, success sometimes seems to come without relationships. Temporary success or short-term success may not, in fact, involve anybody but you. However, long-term success and continued wealth building require people and relationships. Regardless of whether you are investing or if you are building a business, you are going to require key individuals around you who share your goals. These key individuals are the people who make up your team.

Your team members all need to have different and unique skills and talents. Your team will take you farther and keep you there longer than you would by yourself.

Depending on your endeavor, your team may consist of a mentor, an accountant, an attorney, a financial advisor, a real estate agent, a mortgage officer, and an insurance agent among others. In my nine businesses and investing ventures, I have several teams. Some of my team members remain the same and translate from team to team. For example, my accountant and bookkeepers stay the same regardless of whether it's a business or an investment. Some of my mentors also remain the same while I keep others as specialized advisors for specific projects. In my opinion, the two most important people on your team are your accountant and your attorney.

More than likely, your team will need a great attorney, a great accountant and a bookkeeper. There should be a wide variety of people in your team, depending on the nature of the business. In my limousine business, for example, I have two mechanics, a key person at the Ford dealership service department, a key person at the limousine manufacturer, a leather repair individual, a paint-touch up individual, a body shop owner, a specialized insurance agent, the same accountant, the same bookkeeper, a detailing company owner, a different attorney than my normal one, a successful limousine business owner as my key mentor and a lot owner.

> Long-term success and continued wealth building require people and relationships.

One of the best ways to add people to your team is by asking for referrals. Ask people you trust who they have on their teams that you might be able to use also. Don't just take anyone's word for granted, however. Once you have the referral, make sure and do what I call a soft interview.

This is different from the way I find someone when I don't have a referral. If someone was not referred to me, then I interview a total of three individuals who have similar qualifications, and I determine who would be the best suited for my team. When I am referred to someone, though, assuming that my initial conversation with them goes well, and I have a good impression of him or her, I will ask a portion of the same questions I would normally use in an interview and trust that the referral will prove to be valuable. After all, if they don't turn out to be what I was led to expect, I can always interview three others and select one of them.

By the way, as I'm doing this, I'm not promising a position on my team or committing to anything I can't deliver. All I tell them is that I hope to give them future referrals and be a great client and that's enough for them to be excited enough to work with me. I stay true to my word, and if they prove to be valuable and long-term, they earn all of my referrals.

Everyone on your team needs to have the ability to be honest with you. Just because they work for you or are contracted to you, that should not negate their responsibility to be honest. It's up to you to create this atmosphere in the relationship. I know people who have great teams around them, however, the condition for success is that their team members be "yes" people. Having a team around you that always agrees with you, despite feeling they shouldn't move forward, will ultimately result in failure.

Just because someone seems to be difficult or is downright rude, doesn't necessarily mean that you shouldn't add them to your team. Some of my best team members were difficult to deal with at the beginning. In other words, they are so great and so good at what they do that they don't have to have good people skills in order to be successful. That was the case for me on a couple of occasions. I learned to overlook their lack of people skills, and I was able to capitalize on their specialized area of expertise. To this day, both of these individuals are still on my team and we experience a great deal of success working with each other.

For example, when we were purchasing our first limousine from the manufacturer in California, we found that working with them was a real problem at first. It was a big decision for us, and I was the one in charge of doing all of the due diligence to make sure we were buying the limousine from the right manufacturer. Realizing that this was a manufacturer that I was going to be dealing with not only on this purchase but also in the future, I had to find a way to make it go smoothly. In spite of the fact that I really wanted to tell this person what he could do with the limousine he was trying to sell me, I apologized for a misunderstanding and a bad start to a relationship. I then got in touch with his vice-president of operations and told him what a great job this representative was doing in helping me with our purchase. Within two days, the representative became an amazing person to work with and there was no more attitude and no more problems.

Some people might disagree with how I went about this, but I didn't feel I had a choice. This was the best company to deal with according to all of my research, and I would be doing a lot of business with them over a long period of time. I needed to create a great relationship in order to add them to my team. As a result of doing this, we moved forward and purchased our first limousine.

A few weeks later, we experienced some slight problems which, as a result of my relationship with this individual, were fixed in a way that was far above the norm for good customer service.

I know many people who have a temper and the second someone does something to upset them, they vent on them. They believe this is healthy and commands respect. The problem is that they will never build a long-lasting team that will, in turn, insure their success. Had I dealt with this representative the way I wanted to, I would still have purchased the limousine and moved forward. However, in the weeks and in the months to come, I wouldn't have received the kind of service and the discounts that ultimately would further my success in the business.

Purpose to Keep People in Debt to You

Whether you are building your team, building your business or creating wealth and investments, you are going to need to learn how to put people in debt to you. I realize this may sound a little manipulative but it really has to do with your level of service to others before you expect them to serve you in return. You have to first give in order to receive. Putting people in debt to you means that you do anything and everything you can to benefit them first. There are times when people will not reciprocate. This information will be useful, too, since you will then know who is a giver and who is a taker. When you give to a giver, he gives back more. However, when you give to a taker, he will take more.

The Golden Rule says to do unto others as you would have them do to you. It's simply a matter of putting their needs first and your needs second. Maya Angelou said that people will forget what you say. But they will never forget how you make them feel. This is about being genuine and honest in your motives. Otherwise, you're not fooling anybody. You and I both know when someone is doing something with an ulterior motive and wanting something in return.

> **People will forget what you say, but they will never forget how you make them feel.**

I could write a whole book on the benefits of just this one principle. I'll share an example. As we were shopping for a limousine, we began to deal with another local limousine provider that had one for sale. However, we decided to build our own for other reasons, including financial. I felt badly about how this ended up with this individual, so I sent him a note of apology and a gift certificate. A couple of weeks later, I called to see how things were going and if there was anything I could do for him through any of our other businesses.

He began to tell me about a legal problem he was having. Immediately that day, I took care of the issue, which cost me $150. Not fully understanding or realizing the impact this would have, I decided not to ask for any money toward this bill.

As the weeks continued, we kept in touch and eventually had lunch. It started off as a normal lunch, talking about the business and the industry. The legal issue came up again, along with a problem associated with it. I had just gone through a similar situation a few months ago and my attorney solved it for me. Because of my experience, I knew the answer.

He was so overwhelmed with how I wanted to help him that the lunch meeting changed the course of my limousine business forever. At the time, we had been in business for a little over a month, and I realized that we were missing some big pieces to the puzzle. This man offered all of his resources, including his drivers, his training and all of his contacts. As a direct result of his offer, our business began to prosper overnight. It was a total and unexpected surprise. Today we're friends and I'm always checking in with him to see what I can do for him.

This principle is vital to ensuring the success of any business you ever start. Customers and clients need to feel like you've done so much for them that they will never leave you and that they owe you something. Customers and clients are hard to get in the first place so why would you lose them to a competitor and have to replace them? Clients are irreplaceable, no matter how many new clients you get. Think of it this way. You could have had that many more if you had kept the old ones. What level of service do you provide for your clients? Maybe it's the clients that your company pays you to keep happy or maybe it's the clients in your investing or personal business. Either way, they're important.

A year ago I changed my whole business model in my primary business. I decided that I would no longer spend money on advertising. Advertising was expensive and rarely generated leads with people I enjoyed working with. I invested the time that it took to generate new clients to spend it instead with the existing clients. I also spent the dollars that were dedicated to advertising on serving the existing clients.

The results were phenomenal. Today I can really say that I work by referral only and it's the greatest feeling in the world. I'm serving my clients in any way that I can and at any time that they need it. In return, they help me with all the referrals I could ever handle.

At the core of working business by referral is keeping people in debt to you, not so that you can get the referrals but rather because you want to genuinely serve them.

My clients, my friends and my family all benefit from my attitude of service to them. As a result, without me even asking, because they know I invest in real estate and in businesses, I am constantly being given referrals to people and situations that further create wealth in my life.

In most situations and when possible, I involve the person who referred me to that situation as a part of the solution and include them in the financial gain. For example, when I am referred to somebody who is in danger of losing his home because of financial distress, I have another opportunity to put that person in debt to me. The principle never ends. Most of the time, these individuals have already met with other companies and people and realized that they were out for their own benefit. These sharks might take advantage of a few people but in the end, their success will be short-lived because they are manipulative and self-centered.

Seek to benefit others and you will be benefited. Get in the habit of asking the key people in your life a very simple phrase. Ask it at the end of your conversation with them, whether it is in person or on the phone. I believe it is magical in the way that it makes them feel and in the results that you will experience. It's really simple. The phrase is, "Is there anything I can do for you or is there anything that you need?"

Over time, I realized that now most of the key people in my life ask me the same thing at the end of meetings or telephone conversations. Putting people in debt to you will totally change your life. As you give to them, you will reap benefits that you never thought possible and create relationships that last for a lifetime. It's about living a life of service and giving. You will always have more friends, more leads, more business and more investment opportunities than you'll ever be able to keep up with.

Purpose to Think Results

I've heard this statement a thousand times, "It takes money to make money." I don't believe it's true. What it takes to make money is thinking of ways to invest, thinking up new ideas, thinking of ways to solve problems, thinking of how to create relationships and thinking of how to benefit people. These are the keys to producing money.

Money is a result. It's the result that naturally happens when some of these principles are utilized. Of course, we can take examples of how people make money illegally but that's not really relevant because they never get to keep it for any length of time.

Decide and train yourself to think, "How?" Wealthy people and overachievers think about two things. They think about what they want and how to get it. These are the keys to their thinking success. Get in the habit of taking action on good ideas now. Don't delay. Don't wait and don't make the mistake of not writing it down. Every good idea that I have or that my team has, even if it's not the right time, I write it down in my Palm Pilot. And when I write it down, I create an alarm for it to remind me once a month, every three months or however often I need to revisit the issue until the time is right for it.

> **Get in the habit of taking action on good ideas now.**

For example, I knew of a few people who had successful on-line merchandise sales businesses. It was an idea that I enjoyed thinking about, but I didn't know enough about it to do it yet. Every time I spoke to somebody about it, I got the runaround. I didn't know where to start, but I kept the idea active in my mind and kept it at the forefront of future projects I wanted to get involved with.

I began to speak with retailers, manufacturers, wholesalers, and anyone else I thought might help me with information. A year went by and I thought this was not something I could ever wrap my mind around. I took all the information that I had gathered over the year and

I placed it in a memo pad and kept it active on my Palm Pilot. I then created a reminder in my weekly calendar to remind me every Friday to think about anyone else I could talk to who could help identify the missing pieces and start on the process once and for all.

Six more months went by and I had a few conversations with other people but nothing happened. I really wanted to give up, but the reminder every Friday on my Palm Pilot built determination. Shortly after that, I was on a vacation in Cancun and while taking a walk on the beach and talking to somebody about this very issue, the whole idea, the whole system became a reality to me. Maybe it was an epiphany or some kind of a revelation, but it was amazing, to say the least. It made sense and I had the missing pieces I was searching for all this time.

I returned home and for the next ninety days, I created a system and put a team in place. I want you to see that this idea started with, "How can I get in the business of selling merchandise online too?" I knew people were making great money, and I knew it was a great business, and I knew it was a way for me to leverage my time. But I had to keep thinking toward the results and not give up on it.

I now have a few other things that I want to get started on in the area of investing but don't yet know how. But you can be sure that I have active files for them in my PDA and I am thinking, "Results."

Seek ideas, strategies, different ways of doing things and the connections and the people you need will eventually work out. Forget the reasons why it might not happen and focus on when it will eventually happen. Ideas are for taking action. Average people think about all the reasons they may not be successful most of the time. Maybe it's the economy or their lack of education or their current relationships. They blame everything and everyone else for their continued average life. It's up to you to make this change and instead think results. Keep your thoughts focused on what you want and continue to assemble the "how tos" for getting them.

> **Ideas are for taking action.**

Purpose to Have Mentors

At the end of the last chapter, I mentioned a conversation that I had with my mentor, Tom Anderson, aboard a cruise ship on the Mexican Riviera. It was life-changing to say the least. I believe that I was at a crossroads in life that day and getting ready to make a decision and create a lifestyle that could haunt me the rest of my life, one that I would regret at the end of my life. Thankfully, however, the decision I made led to a lifestyle that I would enjoy, that would challenge me and create the life for me and my family that I've always dreamed of.

Having a mentor in your life is absolutely critical to your ability to create wealth and have money work for you. A mentor in your life will challenge you, will inspire you and at times, correct you. You are not an island unto yourself. You're not a lone ranger in this game of building wealth. If you have the mentality that you are going to do it yourself, you're wrong. You might succeed in the short term, but you'll never experience success in the long term.

Building wealth is not just about getting money. Just like an airplane navigator that makes corrections and adjustments in the flight path to arrive at the final destination, we need someone who can be honest and help us see things that we cannot see. A good mentor is not concerned with whether or not your feelings get hurt. A good mentor is concerned with you making bad decisions and hurting yourself.

A mentor is very simply someone you trust, you like and who is genuinely interested in you and your success. This person doesn't have to be a multimillionaire to share and impart into your life. However, I do believe that he or she needs to have a proven track record and be successful in the areas that you're going to ask of them. I would never share my financial situation with someone who earns less than me or who doesn't understand business or investing. That would be foolish.

I have five mentors in my life and they are all critical to my growth in overcoming problems from time to time. I don't go to all five of them and compare notes from the last one I met with. I go to each of them with different issues for the most part.

One of my mentors is Richard Taylor, who is absolutely the best and most phenomenal person I know in the creation and cultivation of relationships. While he has achieved great financial success and success in other areas, I really capitalize on having him teach me how to create long-lasting, beneficial business and personal relationships.

Another one of my mentors is Scot Anderson. In fact, we've become the very best of friends. Like me, Scot is very successful financially in his business endeavors, however, he is the kind of father to his children that I always wanted

> **If you have the mentality that you are going to do it yourself, you're wrong.**

to be to my children. Growing up without a father has left me with little understanding of how to be one. I think it's a positive thing, because I could have just as easily had a horrible father and been scarred by that, too. I talk with Scot about being a parent and everything concerning my family and kids.

Another one of my mentors is Dr. Matt Mannino. He created the single largest privately owned chiropractic firm in the nation and provides me with valuable business knowledge.

Another mentor in my life is Jason Anderson, who is absolutely brilliant when it comes to money, not just because he is the CFO of a major corporation, but because he understands the practical application of values and ethics and morals as it relates to building wealth.

Dr. Tom Anderson and his wife, Maureen, are by far the greatest mentors I've ever had in my life. I don't know what I did to deserve the relationship or the knowledge that they share with me, but I know I wouldn't be where I am if it weren't for them.

Don't limit your mentors. My mentors, in spite of the fact that I go to them for specific things, still have an influence in many other areas of my life. I know them and trust them. They have the freedom to share anything in any area with me that they believe would be of value.

You need to look for people in your life to mentor you. What are some of the qualifications or prerequisites you should consider? The first is that you need to be able to trust them. You need to be able to trust that what they tell you, what they share with you, is in your best interest, not their own.

Secondly, examine their lives before you ask them to teach you anything. The proof is in the pudding. Are they really successful or are they just acting like they are? Talk to the people closest to them without conducting a major investigation. Find out what they are really like when they aren't being watched by a lot of people.

Third, ask yourself if you could see yourself becoming more like that individual in the area you're going to be talking to them about.

I don't make it some weird thing when I ask someone to be my mentor. I just assume that they will be. How I do that is very simple. I start off by making myself valuable to them. I find out what's important to them and how I can help them accomplish their goals. I'm not talking about something big. I'm talking about small things. For example, Dr. Matt realized that I had a great system which allowed me to drive my cars for free. He was already a multimillionaire, but he wanted a Hummer like mine. We talked for a few minutes, and I got to find out what he was looking for in a Hummer. Using my own money, my own time and energy and resources, I went and I found him the vehicle that was absolutely perfect for him. It was priced $3,000 under the going rate and, frankly, I was tempted to buy it myself. I made a contract, wired the money and then I called him and said, "We have a great deal. Would you like me to go pick it up for you? It's out of state."

After the transaction was complete, he was so thankful. I had put earnest money down on the vehicle, but I decided not to bring it up to him. A couple of weeks later, he remembered it anyway and sent the money to me.

The next time I was in his office for an adjustment, he asked me what he could ever do for me. I responded by asking if he would meet me once a month for breakfast or lunch and let me ask a few questions here and there. He was not only happy to do it; he was flattered to be asked. That was the beginning of a great relationship and he knows that I would do anything for him if he ever needed it.

Having mentors will cost you a little money because it's a matter of investment. Life is about investment—investing financially, investing in people, investing in relationships and investing in yourself. Any time I have an opportunity to pay for something for my mentors, I do it. It doesn't matter if it's lunch or something I know they've been wanting. Birthdays, Christmas and other special events are a big deal, and I always make sure that they know I appreciate them. The information and the knowledge that they share with me is invaluable. I couldn't go and read a book about it. I couldn't go to a seminar and get the same information. And so, when I'm with any of them, I'm always looking for opportunities to find out what I can do for them, what's going on in their lives or if they need help with anything. If I discover anything, I solve the problem as soon as possible at no charge and with little consideration for how long it takes. Their problem is my problem. The relationship is a two-way street. You glean information from them and give anything you can back in return.

If you're interested in a long-term relationship with your mentor, then you have to take their advice to heart. I'm not saying you have to do everything they tell you to do or suggest, but if you do just the opposite over and over again, they won't be very excited to invest any more time in your life.

In addition to the mentors you know personally and meet with on a regular basis, there are others that can be a part of your life. Just because you do not know them personally doesn't mean they can't be a mentor to you. For example, I have only met Robert Kiyosaki a few times, and I couldn't say we are friends but I consider him one of my most important mentors. Allow me to qualify this statement. For someone to be a mentor, you simply need to be influenced by their advice and directed into making similar choices that they would make. Because I have read all of his books and choose to put them into practice, that makes him a mentor to me. Reading one of his books and choosing not to practice what he teaches would make him just another author whose book I read.

> Having mentors will cost you a little money because it's a matter of investment.

Purpose-driven wealth means considering what we spoke about in this chapter and incorporating these keys as you begin to build wealth. Deciding upon these things in advance will help to ensure that your success is not short-lived. Purpose to do them.

9

REAL MONEY, REAL TIME WEALTH

E verything we have presented up to this point has been to prepare for this chapter. Examining your belief systems, challenging your current way of thinking, getting a vision for the things you desire and knowing purpose-driven wealth strategies all make up the foundation that you will need to get started, a strong foundation which now empowers you to take action and begin the process of creating wealth.

Over the past three years, I have used this system to earn my first million dollars, working part time, and I have continued building wealth from there. This is not something I just put together or read somewhere. It's been a part of my life for quite some time now. In addition, I have shared several different parts of this system with literally hundreds of people over the last year and have seen it make a great impact on their lives.

I knew when I first stumbled onto the process myself over four years ago that it was going to make all of my goals a reality but at the time, I did not realize it could be taught to others with any real value or consequence. Now that it has proven itself out in my life, I am fully convinced that it carries with it the ability to change anyone's life by placing him or her on the path to creating wealth.

I did not ever imagine that I would be sharing a system with people. However, as I began to write this book and survey different people, I began to realize how many people were ready to build wealth. They had worked on their goals. They had worked on their belief systems. Some had even started to invest in different areas. But the majority of people, were simply not seeing any considerable results because they didn't know what to do next. Their actions were not planned or methodical. They were random at best. That's when it dawned on me how great the value of a system is in people's lives.

Since realizing this, I have organized this process into a methodical and strategic system which I named "The Real Money, Real Time Wealth Creation System." I teach it along with other valuable information at my live wealth-building seminars.

I named it this because the system will produce real money in a real amount of time. It's not a get-rich-quick scheme, pie in the sky or vague innuendos. The Real Money, Real Time Wealth Creation System is about everyday people getting actual results by creating real wealth. It's about getting results in a very short amount of time. While immediate action is required in order to start building wealth today, it's designed to take very little time to get started. Please don't make the mistake of approaching this as new information which you will consider and maybe over a period of time begin to implement. It's time to take action. You are ready. You are prepared, and if you delay action, the chances are that you will never begin. If you've read up to this point, there's no reason why you are not qualified to begin building your wealth now.

My system is broken into three phases that are designed to be completely implemented within a matter of a few weeks with minimal effort—assess, access and accumulate. Assess your life. Access additional cash flow. Accumulate wealth. First, I will share the system outline and then I will discuss each phase in greater detail.

> **The Real Money, Real Time Wealth Creation System** is about everyday people getting actual results by creating real wealth.

The Real Money, Real Time Wealth Creation System

Phase 1: Assess

Assess your future, starting with where you are today.
- Determine what your one-year goals are.
- Create your spending plan, including all expenses and income.

Phase 2: Access

Access additional income to produce cash flow.
- Determine how many extra hours you can commit every week.
- Determine a business that you will start.
- Determine the amount of income the business will earn.

Create the game plan to achieve it.
- Create the plan for where your business income will flow, which is your business spending plan.
- Start an investment account.

Phase 3: Accumulate

Accumulate cash flow, converting it into wealth.
- Create a business entity or entities.
- Convert personal expenses to business expenses.
- Redistribute personal funds to debt elimination, income shortage or investment.
- Reinvest or replace assets to achieve desired cash flow.
- Commit not to increase lifestyle for eighteen months.

Phase 1: Determine what your one-year goals are. Create your budget, including all expenses and income.

Phase 1 is about assessing your current situation based on your personal spending plan. After comparing your one year goals to where you are currently, you will realize if they are achievable. In addition, you will be able to tell if you have extra money or are short of money every month. In the event that you are short, this will be your first priority to correct. If, on the other hand, you have disposable income, you will want to redirect it to produce investment income.

Phase 2: Determine how many hours you will invest into your business.

Phase 2 begins with how many extra hours you can set aside to begin building your wealth. If you are married, make sure and get your spouse's commitment to support this decision. This will help to avoid unnecessary interruptions and increase the overall commitment. If possible, your spouse can support the business by working with you or possibly set aside hours for his or her own business. In either event, at the beginning of this process, you will have to invest yourself. As time goes on and profits increase, you can begin to delegate some of the responsibilities to others.

Determine a business that you will start.

Besides deciding how many hours to invest in your new business, you will now need to determine which business you are best suited to start. Choosing your business begins with first looking at what your skills, talents and desires are. What is the skill set you use for your full-time employment? What are other skills that you possess? A client spoke to me recently about how short he was in his finances. At the time, he was employed with a mortgage company as a computer help desk representative. I asked him a few questions about his skills and talents and it became obvious that computers were his passion. It was simple. He needed to start a computer general help business. I became his first client and gave him an eighty-hour project. From there he told everyone about his business and, after the first couple of months, finding clients was not a problem. Today he has reinvested that business income and not increased his lifestyle, and he continues to build his business besides his full-time job.

Starting your dream business is probably not the first one that you need to start, especially if you have debt and aggressive first-year goals. Your dream business will probably require a great deal of capital and work before you can see any profit. Your first business needs to start generating cash flow within a month. If your game plan does not clearly identify how you can do this, then this is not the business you need to start now. Focus on starting a business that will build wealth quickly and your dream business can follow later. Additionally, what you learn in your first couple of businesses will help you when it is time to build your dream business.

Your dream business and lifestyle will come only after you commit to starting somewhere. A disabled mom was referred to me recently and wanted to get some advice for her and her nineteen-year-old son. She described him as a true entrepreneur but he just wasn't doing so well yet and was becoming very discouraged. The son lived at home, and his mom was pouring her limited income into his business so he could really get it off the ground. I agreed to the meeting and within the first two minutes, it became apparent that the problem was that he started his dream business with no prior experience and a zero financial base from which to do so. He had started a non-profit organization for a cause he had always dreamed of helping. He had little help getting started from a few sponsors and he had already invested quite a bit of money into it. The solution was simple. He needed to have his first business produce cash, invest in assets and then, over time, come back to his non-profit organization.

The number one key to your business is generating cash flow. It doesn't matter what it is. Marketing and sales are your number one priority so that you can keep generating cash flow. Look into flyer companies, marketing companies, telemarketing centers and other companies whose mission is to advertise your business. Call all your friends, family and Christmas card list and tell them you just started your business. Tell them you need their help. Most people are happy to help. If they aren't potential candidates for you, ask them who they might know who is. Offer them a fee for referrals. Post fliers at every possible legal location and price out ads in all kinds of publications. Look into the internet as a viable advertising medium and while you're there, research other methods to advertise and market your new business. Do whatever it takes to find clients for your business.

> **Focus on starting a business that will build wealth quickly.**

Determine the amount of income the business will earn and create the game plan to achieve it.

As we look at starting your business, we need to create the game plan that identifies what needs to happen to earn your desired income, based on your one-year goal. For example, if you decide your new business will earn $1,200 per month, then you will need to figure out how much in sales you need to accomplish that.

Take, for example, a general computer repair business. Assuming that you charge $20 per hour with a $15 trip charge and a three-hour minimum, you will need to obtain four clients a week. Assuming each of the four only keep you for the minimum of three hours, this will be twelve billable hours. Twelve hours times $20 an hour is $240 per week plus four $15 trip charges. This gives a total of $300 per week or $1200 per month. The game plan is simply breaking down your desired monthly cash flow into an achievable, realistic course of action.

Create the plan for where your business income will flow to.

Next, look at where you want your business income to flow. There are three major categories that will make up most business spending plans. The first should be whatever expenses your business requires as operating expenses, including your projected tax liability. The second should be how much you will set aside for building wealth and investing. The third and final category should be debt elimination or meeting any personal spending plan shortages. Remember the difference between bad debt and good debt when compiling these figures.

Start an investment account.

The final step in Phase 2 is to set up an investment account which your business will begin to fund. This is the percentage that you have determined will go to building wealth and investments. This account is strictly used to create wealth and to invest in opportunities. It's not a reward fund, a vacation fund, a bill fund or to be used for anything else. In order to be committed to creating wealth, you need to be committed to protecting the account from which it will originate. For some people, I strongly recommend creating this account in a bank different than their primary bank in order to prevent easy access.

Phase 3:   Create a business entity or entities.

Phase 3 begins with the creation of your company entity like an LLC or some type of corporation. It's absolutely vital that you have an entity to decrease your personal liability and your tax liability.

Convert personal expenses to business expenses.

Now that you have a company, you can begin to transfer current personal expenses that legitimately are being used in your new business, i.e. car payments, car insurance, and cell phone bills. Converting these expenses will now leave disposable income in your personal budget that will now be allocated towards debt payoff or building wealth. Depending on the type of business you create, you will want to see your accountant to discover qualifying current personal expenses that can become your new company's expenses. Remember to ask your accountant if you are allowed to have your new company pay for a portion of your utilities and housing expenses if you have an office in your home. When you convert these expenses, this means that your company checks will be used to service future payments. In addition, depreciation and appreciation may also be used by your accountant to benefit your new company at the end of the year.

Redistribute personal funds to debt elimination, income shortage or investment.

In the event that you have discovered disposable income in your personal spending plan, you will now want to dedicate it to debt elimination, personal income shortage and investment. The same goes for any extra income that has been created from any expenses that have been transferred over to your new business.

Reinvest or replace assets to achieve desired cash flow.

This is the icing on the cake for most people because up to this point by doing the system, they may be earning additional cash flow, have a business and are eliminating debt. However, for some people, they may have several non- or under-performing assets. This might be things like equity in their homes, savings accounts or managed accounts. If you are deciding to create wealth, you will need to be pro-active in managing your own money.

Depending on your one-year goals and your new found cash flow, it is strictly your decision to pull money out of your home or not. Some people are okay with this and others have a strong commitment not to do it. Personally, I only do it when I know where the funds will be committed and I am reasonably sure that it will produce far more than the interest rate and additional payments and any closing costs that will incur in getting the refinance done.

Commit not to increase your lifestyle for eighteen months.

As simple as this sounds, it's imperative that you make this commitment to yourself before you begin. It's going to be very tempting in a few months, when you see how much extra money you are earning and how great you feel about eliminating your debt, to start increasing your lifestyle. All of a sudden, you are able to afford that vacation or the payment on your dream car. It's too soon, though. Remember what the wealthy people do. They allow their wealth to drive their lifestyle. They don't go out too early and begin purchasing liabilities which will hinder their ability to increase their assets.

Your assets need to be able to purchase your liabilities. Harness your new found joy and redirect it to creating more wealth by continuing to invest your money. After your first year, you should have eliminated a portion of your debt, continued to build your business and its cash flow and now you can make modest increases to your lifestyle.

For example, a year after starting my first business, I purchased a car that I always wanted to have. I financed it and had my business pay the majority of the car payments and related expenses. It was, after all, a business tool and one that would increase my personal lifestyle but also would increase the number of clients I would begin to work with.

Let's begin to talk about how the system works practically in everyday life. In an effort to keep the system simple and easy to follow, I will be sharing the simulated example of a below average couple with no assets and negative cash flow.

For our hypothetical couple, she is a college professor and he is an aviation mechanic. They have two children.

Phase 1: Their goals are:
- To pay off $12,000 in consumer debt,
- To pay off their vehicle ahead of schedule,
- To add $800 a month to their income,
- To purchase their first home within twelve months,
- To begin to accumulate long-term wealth.

Their current spending plan:
- They have no extra income and in fact are short $300 a month. They have been using credit cards to hide the shortage.
- They have no assets, no home equity and no 401(k) accounts, savings accounts, mutual funds or IRAs.

Phase 2: Determine how many hours they will invest into their businesses:
- She is able to commit to ten to twelve additional hours per week.
- He is able to commit to twenty additional hours per week.

Determine a business to start:
- Given what they do for a living and because he is very good at working on cars in addition to aircraft, he decides that he will begin to work on cars by starting a service as a traveling mechanic.
- She will start an after-hours and weekend tutoring service.

Determine the amount of income the business will earn and create the game plan to achieve it:

Creating the game plan determines whether the one-year goals are achievable. If, for example, they wanted to have a house in six months, an extra $4,000 a month and totally pay off their debt, it wouldn't be achievable because the game plan wouldn't be realistic.

The business needs to earn an additional $2,500 per month.

- His plan, based on their goals, will be that he needs to charge $20 an hour, plus a $15 trip charge within a twenty mile radius, excluding the cost of parts. That will mean that he needs to find fifteen hours of work to perform plus the drive time, which would equal twenty hours a week. Earning $20 per hour times fifteen hours a week is $300 plus an estimated four trip charges per week, bringing the total to $360 per week or $1,440 per month.

- She will require eleven students a week at $25 per hour, which will produce $275 per week or $1,100 per month.

Create the plan for where the business income will flow to:

Based on a total of $2,500 per month in business income, they will set aside 30% ($750) for taxes and business expenses, 50% ($1,250) for wealth building and investing and the remaining 20% ($500) for debt elimination.

Start an investment account:

They start an investment account and begin to funnel their 50% into this account.

Phase 3: Create business entities:

They each create two corporations and designate them as S corporations.

Convert personal expenses to business expenses:

Looking over what current items are now used for business, they begin to transfer the cell phones, their car payment and car insurance to their new companies. A good accountant is able to count these as legitimate company expenses while discounting an accurate percentage for personal use.

Redistribute personal funds to debt elimination or investment:

By converting the car payment, the car insurance and the cell phones from the personal spending plan to the company spending plan, this creates a surplus of $625 per month. This amount is now committed to paying off their debt quicker and to meeting the existing $300 a month shortage in their personal spending plan.

Reinvest or replace assets to achieve desired cash flow:

They have no real assets to reinvest, so no action is required in this step.

Let's wrap it all up. They started out being short $300 every month and they had $12,000 in consumer debt. They started with the following goals:

• To pay off $12,000 in consumer debt,
• To pay off their vehicle ahead of schedule,
• To add $800 in monthly income,
• To be able to purchase their first home within twelve months,
• To finally begin to accumulate long term wealth.

To pay off the $12,000 debt and eliminate the $300 a month shortage, they add $625 per month to their personal budget by converting existing personal expenses to business expenses. Three hundred dollars of this goes toward their existing shortage, leaving $325, which is dedicated to paying off their $12,000 debt. They also combine their current monthly debt payments with the additional $500 per month from their businesses. Taking the total of these three amounts, they are able to completely pay off the debt in twelve months.

Their goal of paying off their vehicle early has also been achieved, though a little differently than they expected. Their vehicle is transferred to the business and because it is no longer a personal debt but rather a company expense, it no longer is necessary to pay it off early. However, it could easily be done by allocating some percentage of the company income to doing this, if desired.

The goal of $800 in monthly income is accomplished in the second month of their business by committing $1,250 of business income to their investment account. Notice that the original goal was to obtain an extra $800 in income but the mindset must be to take all extra income and begin to invest it.

The goal of purchasing their first home in twelve months is also easily met by taking the $1,250 each month from the business account and placing it into an investment account which equals $15,000 in twelve months. I personally consider homes that you live in and that increase in value and appreciation to be assets and therefore qualify to be purchased out of an investment account. Therefore, this $15,000 can be used for a down payment. I would highly recommend doing a no down mortgage loan and having the seller pay for all closing costs. This would result in having this $15,000 to invest in other places. Doing this, they will have $15,000 working for them in addition to the growing equity in their new home.

> **Now it is time to start investing this money, using your team as resources and guides.**

The goal of accumulating long-term wealth is now in action on many levels. Twelve short months later, their personal spending plan has an extra $325 per month, plus the consumer debt minimum payments which no longer have to be made. Their business spending plan has the $1,750 ($1,250 wealth building and $500 debt payoff which was already accomplished) in cash flow. The combined total of these two equals $2,075 a month that should continue to go to their investment account. Assuming they do not use the $15,000 they had set aside in their investment account for their new home, this could be allocated to begin investing. Be sure to plan the most effective method for taking business funds when they are used for personal debt and personal investments as these are not actual business expenses. Your accountant can help you determine this. It might be by taking the money as a salary or some other method.

Now it is time to start investing this money, using your team as resources and guides to generate even more wealth. The initial business income is great to begin with, but now it's time to increase that amount and place even more into the investment account. When I first got started, I was only placing $800 a month into my investment account. Today, this amount has grown dramatically. It is still being placed into my investment account. Money now really does work for me and it will work for you as you stay committed to increasing your deposit amount into your investment account.

Take the money you accumulate in your investment account and begin to invest it into other new businesses, inventions, ideas, stocks, self-directed mutual funds, real estate and other investments. The possibilities are endless. Do your research and figure out the numbers for yourself before making investments. Businesses and real estate are two of my favorite ways to generate wealth. If you desire monthly cash flow, purchase real estate properties that generate monthly cash flow. If, on the other hand, you prefer money in lump sums, begin to search and work on homes you can purchase and resell in a shorter amount of time. Work within your team to accomplish your specific goals. Everyone is different in their desires and comfort levels.

Considering the couple we just spoke about, I want to point out how much faster their wealth creation process would have been if they had some assets to work with, such as equity in their home. It would have been much easier and faster if they had liquid assets. In this case, I would advise to reinvest this money into higher producing investments such as income-producing real estate or other investments. Having something to convert is always easier but sadly, in many people's financial lives today, that simply is not an option. In either event, as you can see, the wealth creation process is simple and achievable.

Making a commitment not to increase your lifestyle and to stay on track with building wealth is absolutely essential. If there was ever a time anyone would want to buy a new car or bigger home, this would be it because there is extra money and there is a new business generating cash flow. Establish building wealth first for a period of time before even thinking about upgrading your lifestyle. Decide to get out of the rat race once and for all by having your money start working for you. Allow your assets and investments to purchase your liabilities and gradually increase your lifestyle.

I currently own thirteen properties, including my own personal one, and while I could afford to purchase my next dream car, which is a Ferrari, and I could afford to live in my 9,000 square foot dream home, it simply isn't time yet. The reason is simple. My assets and investments cannot pay 100% for these items just yet, and until they do, we are committed to continue building wealth. This commitment will insure that we will not have to wait for very long at all.

Winners are in the habit of taking action. Research has been done that compares losers and winners and the key difference is in how fast winners take action. Successful people keep taking action over and over again and they succeed while others around them accuse them of being lucky. Take action now to start building wealth and start doing the system. The longer you wait, the more the probability increases that you will never take action.

10
GETTING DOWN TO BUSINESS

I think there are turning points and certain memories that are ingrained in the mind of a child forever. I remember when I was thirteen years old and had just finished eating all that there was to eat for dinner. I was still pretty hungry.

To get my mind off the hunger, I decided to get my clothes out for school the next day. I realized that the flap to my Converse tennis shoe had become detached. I had just glued it the week before. As I was going to a different room to find the glue, out of the corner of my eye, I noticed a family eating at the Dairy Queen right in front of my house. Their table seemed to be covered with food.

I can still remember the feeling of jealousy and anger that surged through me and how I wondered why they got to eat until they were full and I was still hungry. I made the decision right then that I would never be poor again.

Of course, I couldn't do anything about it until I grew up. But it felt good anyway to make a decision to never be hungry again. I didn't care. I was mad at not having enough food, living in a shack and always wearing hand-me-downs that didn't fit right.

Even though I hated poverty, I didn't have the tools to overcome it. It's not enough to desire or want something. If you don't have practical application of that desire in the form of an action plan, then that desire becomes a hallucination.

Starting a Business to Increase Cash Flow

The tool, as discussed in my system, is based upon increasing cash flow. I believe the best way to increase your cash flow begins with the creation of your own business.

I know that anyone can start a business. Anyone who has the desire to build wealth also has the capacity to do it. I don't care if it's going to garage sales and buying used items, cleaning them up a bit and reselling them. It doesn't matter. It costs less than $300 to start a business in most states. Not everybody has money or assets available to them, but most are probably able to assemble $300. Starting a business is accessible to everyone, which is why I believe it is the first step to getting started. You may not have investment money, but a business can generate cash flow within the first few weeks.

Starting a business doesn't take formal education or a wide background of experience. Many successful people have done very well in business without ever finishing school or receiving a college degree. Consider this small list of examples:

Bill Gates founded Microsoft.
Thomas Edison founded General Electric.
Ted Turner founded CNN.

Steve Jobs founded Apple Computers.
Michael Dell founded Dell Computers.
Ralph Lauren founded Polo.
Henry Ford founded Ford Motor Company.

If you look at the statistics, it is the entrepreneurs who make up the greatest percentage of wealth in America today. Owning your own business truly is the American dream.

Up to this point, we've only spoken about starting your first business yourself. But I want to introduce to you the concept of working with others in several businesses. As I mentioned, I have nine businesses. Obviously, I can't do all of them by myself without going crazy. If I did, I wouldn't expect any real results. Therefore, I only focus on my primary business and have developed this system for the others.

In the last year, I had an idea that I have been working on that has proven itself to be very profitable in my life. Very simply, it is finding others who are passionate about a certain business and helping them to achieve their goals. I have partnered with others by providing the initial capital and other resources to get the business going. While we are equal partners, my initial participation was to launch the business. These individuals are then running the day-to-day operations until such a time as we can hire someone to take their place. The goal is to create a business system rather than a situation where one of us has to show up to get paid.

Besides the initial time it takes to start the business, I dedicate an hour or two a month to review and plan with my partners about ways to increase profits. My partners are not disappointed and don't feel that I'm not pulling my end of the bargain. After all, in some cases, if it weren't for me, they wouldn't have a business at all. I gave them the idea, funded the creation of the business and hired the necessary people to get the job done. To me, this is even more fun than investing in other ways because I'm investing in people and I'm investing in ideas.

Of course, you have to be careful with whom you are investing and how the company is working. There are a lot of horror stories about failed businesses and bad partnerships. However, if you take the necessary steps and precautions to set up the company your way and to use your attorney and your bookkeeper, and you have a clear partnership agreement, you greatly reduce the risks. In all the businesses, I have my accountant and my bookkeeper doing all the record-keeping and bookkeeping. I get one simple report every month concerning all the businesses, the cash flow and the profit and loss statements.

Take calculated risks when you're starting a business. Understand what it takes to fully launch and understand what is at stake if it doesn't work. I generally do not dedicate more than $5,000 to $10,000 in starting a business, so my risks are leveraged over a greater number of them. If I'm going to invest more than this amount, it will require a lot more of my attention and focus to ensure that the business runs smoothly and correctly.

At a conference in Hawaii, I met an individual who spends one hour a day, five days a week with his CEO, who runs his 700-employee company in Arizona. He rarely visits his own company because he is managing it through his CEO. This is a large scale example of what I'm talking about, but it starts with doing what you know.

> **In your daily activities, be on the lookout for people who have a great idea.**

In your daily activities, be on the lookout for people who have a great idea or who are already doing a business in which you can join forces with them and take it to the next level. I had a friend who had a home-based business earning $2,000 a month. The problem was that he was working fifteen to twenty-five hours a week to do it. He was happy, but he realized that if he didn't work the business, he wouldn't earn the money. If you remember, this is how we defined self-employed. One day over lunch, we began to talk about the possibility of joining forces so that he could use my funding to hire two employees and improve the business operation.

We became official partners and created an S corporation together. Today he is beginning to work fewer hours and we are making more money together. In addition, he had been a sole proprietor and now he is enjoying the benefits that go along with owning a corporation. He already had a great idea. He had a great business. He just needed a system to take it to the next level.

You can also look for people who have a great idea but who haven't started their business yet. They, more than anybody, would love to have your help so that they can get their business started. All you need to do is cover the minimal costs to get it going.

By starting your first company, you set yourself on the path of a business owner and starting business after business gets easier with each new project. The more you are doing, the better you will get at doing it. Starting your first company is not only about gaining cash flow to build wealth, but it's also about gaining the experience that you're going to need in the future.

Besides partnering with others in creating businesses, think of ways in which you can build your own business by hiring subcontractors to work for you. In my primary business, during a brainstorming session, my wife had the idea two years ago to search for associates who would take my referrals. I would then earn a certain percentage and in exchange they would be on call and available to handle my referrals.

My business was becoming busier and I needed help. I couldn't find anyone else to hire because they wanted salary plus commission and it wasn't feasible. I finally found someone and offered them free use of a new car that I had bought using my car system. I paid for the insurance and they were happy to drive a brand new car with no insurance costs and no car payment. In return, they would work referrals for me. Besides the money that I had to tie up to purchase the vehicle and the low cost of insurance, there was really no real cost to me. It was a mutually beneficial relationship that earned both of us additional income.

I knew some of the people I got into business with better than others but in every case, I have a rule that I never break. Written agreements protect friendships. I put everything in writing and I encourage you to do the same. Discuss and decide every potential situation or problem that could arise and find its solution. Put the terms together that apply to your business before you take it to an attorney. This will save you time and money but more importantly, it will insure that all the items are covered. I always have an attorney draw up the final documents. It's worth it to me to spend $200 to $400 to be sure that everything is done absolutely correctly.

How to Create Business and Cultivate Great Ideas

Hopefully by now you've decided what your business will be but if you haven't, here are some ideas to get you going. In addition, these also could be great second, third and fourth businesses if you find the right people to help you with them. Look on the internet. Do keyword searches. Buy magazines, books and attend good seminars. There are literally hundreds and hundreds of business opportunities to get involved with.

I generally stay away from companies selling businesses that require up-front fees. There are too many other great businesses in which I don't have to pay anybody to get started. If you do pay up-front fees, be careful and do your research.

And don't forget to negotiate. Everything is negotiable. If a company wants a certain amount, leverage your risk. Tell them you want to break it up into a few payments. That way, you make sure that what they're promising is real, and you may only lose one payment if it doesn't work.

My wife and I are friends with a couple who decided that they would open their own business. She enjoyed reading books. Our friend began to purchase books at a low price from secondhand stores and other similar places. She then began to resell them and now earns in excess of $3,000 a month doing it.

Another way that you can begin to cultivate fresh business ideas and even inventions is to handpick a small group and meet with them every week. I am involved with a group of three men that meet once a week for lunch. The purpose of the meeting is simple—to create, to discuss and to implement great ideas and/or inventions. We leave with homework and we come back with results every week. We divide the work evenly. I'm primarily responsible for the legal and the accounting aspect while another one is more adept at the actual market research. Another owns a web design firm and is able to quickly come up with marketing solutions.

Be careful who you have on your team or with what group you participate. I trust all three of these men with my life and we can freely discuss ideas and inventions and I know that not one of them is going to go and take advantage of our ideas individually. It really is a powerful way to develop great ideas and great inventions and get results.

I want to charge you with a new mission. Your mission in life, now that you have begun the Real Money, Real Time Wealth Creation System, is to create, cultivate and implement new ideas. I listen to an average of ten hours a week of teaching CDs. All I'm looking for is one idea that I can use to make thousands of dollars, or stream line my operations, eliminate stress or create a better life for myself and my family. The search for ideas is worth its weight in gold. Subscribe to good financial magazines. Read books and attend quality seminars/conferences to get ideas and be around the people who have them.

11

REAL EQUITY IN REAL ESTATE

Financial literacy is a lifelong pursuit and in the area of real estate, it is something that requires you to stay current with the trends and the market, which often change. Therefore, you have to keep up with what the market is doing in your area, especially as it relates to the values and the predictions concerning future employment and how many people are moving into your city or state.

Research the numbers, develop your team and research the Census Bureau. There you can find out what they're predicting the population will be in five, ten or fifteen years.

The number one rule of real estate is **LOCATION**. It is certainly true in Arizona where I live. Builders started several new home communities very far east and some very far south. They offered excellent prices. When they began to build these homes, initially they created a real buzz for people wanting to move out there. A buyer could acquire a larger home and extra bedrooms for 20% and sometimes 35% less.

People began to move out there a few years ago by the thousands. Everybody thought the communities were going to be awesome. It wasn't that the products, the homes, were not good. The areas had beautiful parks.

Stores eventually came in. Commercial centers popped up and eventually the residents didn't have to drive forty minutes to a grocery store or to do other shopping.

However, the gas prices in Arizona, much like other places in the country, began to skyrocket. People quickly realized that they had made a mistake. It was costing them more and more money to commute back and forth to work. Besides the gas prices, people who bought in these communities began to grow tired of the long drive, the congested traffic and began returning to more centrally-located areas.

Less than two years later, after everybody moved out there, the area began to stagnate and homes were not selling. There were cheap rentals, and resale property prices were driven down. People began to move out of those areas by the hundreds. They moved closer to their jobs, and they began to value the closer areas.

These areas I have mentioned have been some of the hardest hit in terms of prices, not only because of the location but also due to the competing builders who are able to offer huge incentives and discounts that compete with the resale market. The zip code that I live in posted an increase in equity while in some of these areas posted decreases in equity. The only time I don't live by the rule of the best location is when the numbers make sense and it's a great investment.

Location is the number one rule of real estate because people always want to live in great locations. Typically, you will pay a little more for a house in a greatly desired location. And you may even get a smaller house for the money, but in the end, I believe you'll have the upper hand in the better location.

Another thing you need to be aware of is the fact that you should never fall in love with a piece of property before you buy it. If you fall in love with a piece of property before you buy it, you will probably pay way more than it may be worth. First be a smart consumer, then you can create a home that you love.

We look at the numbers first and then we make a financially-educated decision. We don't allow minor or cosmetic repairs to distract us from making good financial decisions. In fact, my wife is an unbelievable interior decorator.

> **Location is the number one rule of real estate because people always want to live in great locations.**

She has ideas that few people have, and she causes the homes we live in to appreciate more than we originally anticipated. She does things for pennies on the dollar, and I couldn't love it more.

I'm trying to talk her into writing a book on interior design. Instead of calling it *Design on a Dime*, we would call it *Design for a Million*. My wife has the uncanny ability to look past all the things a home may need and see the finished product.

I want to take an opportunity in this chapter to discuss a few of the things that you may want to consider when investing in real estate. Before you invest in anything, especially real estate, make sure that you have your team in place. In addition, pay attention to the numbers, and make sure you are making a decision based on financial literacy.

Donald Trump strongly recommends in his book *Think Like a Billionaire*, to always use a realtor when buying real estate. I couldn't agree more. Choose your realtor carefully. I always recommend that you find one that is also a real estate investor. Typically, realtors are paid for by the seller of a property and therefore you, as the buyer, will receive their services at no charge to you. In addition, when you go through a realtor, they have a series of disclosures and several inspections that are designed to help protect you from making a bad choice. Once you find a realtor, you will have a professional representing your interests and someone who can help you verify that the numbers work in your favor.

There are many great ways to invest in real estate. It's up to you to find the method that works best for you and that will work well within your game plan. I have included a few ways I've used to invest in real estate in the following sections. Depending on your own goals, you may need to add some specialists to your team.

As we talked about in previous chapters, a bad real estate market is actually a great opportunity. Generally speaking, in a bad market, there are more homes for sale than there are buyers. This creates a unique and great opportunity for you as an investor. Because there are a lot of sellers trying to sell their homes, there will typically be a lot more deals available. Not only can you negotiate and get a better price on a home, but you may also be able to get financing terms that you normally would not be able to get in a regular market. Remember, the sellers have to compete with other sellers to sell their homes and they want their homes sold. That's why it's for sale.

Everybody has different reasons for wanting to sell. Your job is to find the sellers who really need to sell and make it work for the two of you. In addition, in this market, there may be an increase of people who are not able to make their payments resulting in foreclosures. Do your research and have your team help you to locate some of these individuals or investigate for you how you would be able to go about purchasing foreclosures or pre-foreclosures.

Depending on your area, lease purchasing may be a great way to invest. It's basically the combination of a renter and buyer. Typically, you can collect a couple of thousand dollars as a non-refundable deposit towards the purchase of the home. Additionally, you can either preset the future purchase price or have it be dependent on getting an appraisal done.

I have personally done this quite a bit. I have purchased homes and then obtained a lease purchase buyer. In some cases, the lease purchaser came to me in advance and asked me to purchase the home, using my name and credit and then we went shopping for a home that they wanted. The benefit of doing this is that you are in complete control of the home because it's in your name and they are making the majority or all of the mortgage payments.

When it's time to sell, you typically earn the majority of the appreciation. In some situations, you may want or need to offer the lease purchaser a credit of some of the rental payments or their down payment towards the purchase price. It depends on your market and what is normally customary. In addition, another advantage of lease purchasing compared to leasing is that typically, you can have them be responsible for their own repairs, since they are essentially renting to own.

Have your attorney, who should be on your team by now, do your first lease purchase agreement and provide you a template so that you can use it in the future with different properties that have the same basic terms and conditions. On a final note, I would recommend having a professional property manager be responsible for collecting the rents and managing the property.

Something that has become popular in Arizona has been buying homes when there are renters already included with them. These homes are being sold for average prices but the key is that they come with an existing renter and rental income. You want to make sure that the current renter has an up-to-date lease agreement and you will want to verify when it expires. You need to understand that you are assuming this lease agreement and cannot make any changes to it. This can be a great way of investing because, in the event that you have a tenant who has eighteen months remaining on his lease, you can purchase the home knowing that the renter will make the majority of your mortgage payments for eighteen months. At that point, you can sell the property if there's enough equity to do so, or you can re-rent or lease purchase it to someone else while you're waiting for the equity to build, depending on what your game plan is.

The very first investment home I purchased was from a wholesaler. Most major cities have people who call themselves wholesalers. These individuals have methods of buying homes for way under market value. They can buy them at the courthouse steps via a foreclosure sale or they may have a system of identifying distressed sellers who are in need of selling their home right away. Be careful. Wholesalers will say that their home is worth a lot more than it really is. Don't completely discount them. They may in fact have opportunities where genuine money can be earned. Ask your realtor about finding these individuals or pick up real estate magazines. The better ones will have ads in there. If that doesn't work, they will definitely have ads in magazines and publications directed specifically at realtors.

I have recently added a company to my team that purchased an internet franchise that specializes in receiving information from distressed sellers. I met with them for lunch and have contracted to be the first person they call when a good deal pops up. How they work is that before they even close, they want an upfront fee for their service of assigning a contract to me. Before I pay them anything, they have already obtained a contract signed by themselves and the seller with all the terms and conditions already outlined. I am simply assuming their position as the original buyer in agreeing to execute the exact same terms and conditions that they agreed to.

I've done my research and I have a few others whom I trust verifying the deal. Furthermore, I will verify the potential equity before I pay them for the contract, so I'm fine with paying the fee. Take the time, if you find similar people in your marketplace, to not only ensure that they are legitimate, but also to build a relationship with them so that you can add them to your team.

I mentioned the term "assigning," which, if you are writing purchase offers to buy homes for investment, I suggest always including so that it remains an option for you. It may differ in your area but in Arizona I would write my name, a comma, and then the words "and or assignee or nominee." This tells the seller that I am buying it for now, however, I have the right to assign it to some other buyer before it closes or I can nominate another buyer. Check with your realtor to be sure of the details for your state.

In Arizona, and I would imagine in other parts of the nation, in the event that another buyer takes your position, the original terms and conditions of the purchase contract cannot be altered in any way. This has been invaluable to me, especially when we were investing in vacant land. At times the financing or terms we depended on from a lender would fall through, and we could then simply assign it to someone else in or outside our group, thereby keeping some of our interest and not forfeiting large sums of earnest money. I've also seen a lot of people use this technique to initially purchase a home and then find another investor to take their position. This is their game plan and they make their money when they assign it to someone else, typically by earning a referral fee or perhaps being included in the profit sharing of the property.

Investing in land has been one of my favorite methods of investing in real estate. There are a couple of things you want to be aware of, however, and a couple of things you want to avoid, in my opinion. Be aware of areas with nice custom homes either being built or planned for later. Before I invest in an area, I generally like to see a couple of the custom homes already built so that this gives me an idea of what the area is going to look like and also how large the homes will be. By doing this, I am then able to forecast a price per square foot for the home and determine an assessed value on the land and where it might go in the future.

> Investing in land has been one of my favorite methods of investing in real estate.

Here in Arizona, there are a couple of key subdivisions that meet this prerequisite and in addition to it, offer great views. These areas, as I've discussed previously, are in the best locations and will always be in high demand. Before making a final purchase, ask from the developer the CC&Rs, which outline the rules and restrictions in the subdivision. This information includes things like how big a home can be and whether or not a second story or a basement will be allowed. Also, unless one has been done that you can trust and can verify, you will want to do a survey on the lot in which you are interested.

Beware of purchasing in a subdivision that has not had utilities run to it yet, a subdivision that is incomplete and unincorporated county land. Unless you're very good at and understand the utility process, which I don't, you need to consider this. Regardless of your knowledge, or lack thereof, you definitely want to do your research and have hard numbers before you get involved. Running utilities and services to raw land can be a gamble at times.

If you want to purchase a lot in an incomplete subdivision, make sure that you do your research to find out who the developer is. Sometimes developers get started in a subdivision and for whatever reason, don't finish it or delay the project for several years. In either case, it's not good for your investment. In order to find out who that person is, use your team to do a little research and if you get involved at an early stage, consult your real estate attorney to find out the worst case scenarios.

The next thing I would be very careful of is purchasing raw county land. The reason is simple. In most cases, there are no comparables to go by to determine future value. Your area may be different, but in Arizona, you might invest in a parcel of land, get a great deal on it and then, two months later have neighbors move in with five different manufactured homes right next door to you. As you can imagine, I have a difficult time trying to convince someone to build their multimillion dollar dream home when their neighbors paid $50,000 for theirs. There is no HOA or other restrictions that would prohibit the neighbors from doing a lot of things that could potentially hurt the value of your property.

You don't have any control over the comparables in these areas because you don't know what may happen in the future in unincorporated county parcels of land. I'm not saying you should never buy these. Just buy them with the end in mind for use in a different game plan. One of my great friends and clients realized that a huge golf course was being developed, and he contacted the owner of the raw, unincorporated land across from the future course and negotiated $40,000 an acre. The owner was out of state and was

> **Regardless of your knowledge, or lack thereof, you definitely want to do your research.**

not aware of the incoming golf course. Sure, it was a little risky, especially if the golf course didn't go through, but $40,000 an acre was still a pretty good deal. Needless to say, he's done very well in the project.

Talk with your realtor about how to get the information on all of the sellers whose properties have recently expired and never sold. These can be potentially great investment opportunities because they probably still want to sell and for whatever reason, it hasn't happened yet. It could be an opportunity for you to have your realtor or yourself contact them and make them a reasonable offer.

Most counties in the United States have a problem collecting real estate taxes. When people default for a certain length of time, the county begins to sell back-owed taxes as tax liens. Once you purchase them, you will earn a certain interest rate when the owner of the property finally pays what is owed. In the event that the owner does not pay the taxes, depending on the county, you may even be awarded the property for which you paid the lien. Tax liens are guaranteed to be paid against the property by which they are secured.

Another option is the purchasing of new homes that have never been lived in or that will be constructed for you by a builder. As a general rule, these homes appreciate at a faster rate than re-sales. Again, it depends on the location of the subdivision and some other factors which your realtor can help you with, but generally these can be great investments and homes to live in. If you contract with a builder to build your home, you will have anywhere from eight months to sometimes as long as eighteen months of equity built up without making any monthly payments other than your earnest money and whatever the builder requires up front.

Typically, builders will not give you additional incentives if you are doing business by yourself without your realtor and even if they do, it's never worth it in my opinion. The reason is simple. The builder representative works for the builder. That is his employer. When it comes to looking out for their best interests as opposed to yours, who do you think he will be loyal to? In the event that there is a discrepancy, a problem or an issue against the builder's representative or the builder, it will be you against them and all of their extensive resources. Sure, the builder may be interested in providing good customer service; however, who do you think will probably win this battle if it has to be fought?

I've seen this happen and the buyer has no other recourse but to concede or to cancel and forfeit the earnest money. In most cases, they have a list of people just waiting for you to cancel. If you, as the buyer, however, are purchasing the home through the services of a professional realtor, you are now represented by a realtor that the builder is paying. I realize that builders aren't excited to pay other realtors when they can pay their own field representative, but the reality is that you have to do what's best for you and represent your interest first.

Now if there is a problem or a dispute, you have your realtor and his broker attorney and extensive resources on your side to help make sure that you are represented accurately. It's a no-brainer to me. I'm taking calculated risks in everything that I do. I don't believe in taking any risk if I don't have to and especially if it doesn't cost me anything to totally avoid it. I am not knocking builders in general. For the most part they are great and you may never have a problem with them, but why take a chance?

Regardless of what method you choose to invest in real estate, if you are purchasing a home, I recommend you do the following things. The first is to always purchase a home warranty. In the case of a resale, typically, the home warranty would be paid for by the seller. Ask your realtor to make sure that you are getting the most comprehensive home warranty available. Make a note to yourself to renew that warranty twelve months after you purchase your home. A good home warranty covers all the appliances, heating and cooling, some electrical plumbing and other areas. It's well worth the average cost of $500 a year.

In addition, get in the habit of asking the seller to give you all of their appliances. Typically, sellers are ready to move on and will include them at no charge. Even if they are not advertising it, most are willing to provide you all of their appliances at no cost in exchange for selling their home.

If cash flow is important to you, one of the things you can do, depending on the state in which you live, is to ask the seller to pay for all of your closing costs by raising the price of the purchase contract. The seller then pays for them at the time of closing. You are basically paying for them but you are financing them into your loan, which keeps the money in your pocket for renovations and anything you might need to do with your new property. In addition, this causes the purchase price to be higher by the amount of closing cost, added to the amount that you are financing. This in turn may help you in the future to provide higher comparables to the area for refinancing purposes and resale value.

One thing I would consider most of the time, especially when dealing with vacant land, is to always include in the purchase contract the ability to extend the close of escrow date by at least two weeks. I typically offer a small amount of money in the event and at the time I need this so that the seller is willing to provide it. Depending on the purchase price, somewhere around $500 to $2,000 for this extension is a good deal for the seller and may save me a lot more money in the event there is a problem along the way that delays the closing.

On a final note, regarding any real estate you own, maintaining your properties is the key to insuring that they continue to look the very best they can, resulting in the very highest possible profit. In all of the properties that I own, someone on my team visits them regularly. We make a note of anything big or small that has to be done. We then have people on our team such as general repair individuals, handymen and specific contractors who go and repair those things immediately.

> I don't believe in taking any risk if I don't have to and especially if it doesn't cost me anything to totally avoid it.

On my own personal home, I have a general handyman who comes by the same time every month, and we have a list waiting for him. My wife and I, as we notice little things, keep a running list of all the items in my PDA that have to be addressed the next time he comes by.

Think of your properties the way your next buyer will think of them. When you walk onto a property as a buyer, you don't want to see mismatched paint, faded paint, missed paint spots, broken handles, broken knobs, flooring issues, small drywall issues, bad landscaping, cracked windows, filthy ceiling fans, cobwebs in the corner or any of the other dozens of items that are easy to fix. These things are all too often easy to postpone. Just like you, potential buyers will take note of those items and it will dramatically affect the price and the terms that they will offer you.

If you let enough little things go in your property, it is really hard and expensive to take care of them all at once. Get in the habit of always looking for all the little things that are sure to make a big difference. By doing this, you will command the best terms and highest price possible when you do decide to finally sell, not to mention how much more enjoyable it will be owning the property in the meantime.

Maintain Good Credit

I want to take this opportunity to discuss your credit, which is vital to real estate investing. It's so important to maintain good credit. If you don't, you'll end up paying so much more money in interest and other related fees. It will cost you untold hundreds of thousands of dollars in your lifetime to not protect and maintain your credit and to keep it high.

One of the biggest keys to maintaining your credit has to do with your revolving accounts such as your credit cards. It's been estimated that approximately 40% of your credit score is based on these revolving accounts. Many people are not aware that their revolving accounts have such a great impact on the overall credit score. Other than having derogatory information being reported, this is the single most important aspect you have to be aware of.

The lower the outstanding balances are in your accounts, the higher your scores. As a general rule of thumb, zero to 30% of the available credit limit as your balance results in the highest scores. After I learned this,

REAL EQUITY IN REAL ESTATE 183

I made it a point to always pay off any balance over 30% before the account cycles. By doing this, I am assured that when it reports to the Credit Bureau, it will reflect a 30% or less balance outstanding, causing my credit to stay very high. This is a huge key because if you do not do this, the high balance will stay on your credit report until the next time they report.

For example, let's assume you have a $3,000 VISA and you charge close to the limit every month but you also pay it in full every month when the statement comes in. The problem is that the VISA company is reporting to the Credit Bureau that you consistently come close to maxing your card most of the time. If you were to simply find out when your account cycles by calling them, you could get the payment in before it cycles so that when they do report to the Credit Bureau, they would report a zero balance and still show the account very active.

Ideally, it's recommended that you keep three to five active revolving accounts. If you have older accounts that you are not using, I would suggest not closing the accounts. Keep them active and in good standing and they will help you by providing you with older accounts on your record. Having newer accounts with continually high balances can keep your credit scores low indefinitely, in some cases, even as much as fifty to a hundred points, depending on various factors.

There are a lot of companies out there that say they will repair your credit in exchange for an upfront fee, but be very careful. The majority of these companies are not interested in fixing credit at all as much as they are in collecting money. Refer to your team and do your research before you hire anybody to help you with your credit. There are some good people and there are good companies out there. You just have to find them.

In summary, as you begin to invest money from your investment account, you want to rely on your team to help guide you. When you are first starting out, you are probably not going to feel totally comfortable and that's normal. Rely on your research and what the numbers say in order to insure that you are making decisions that are based on financial literacy.

12
SEE YOU AT THE TOP

Congratulations! You've finished the book. But don't let that be the end of it. You now have all the tools you are going to need to create wealth. It's time to get out there and put the things you've learned into practice. Keep learning and keep growing.

I want to take this opportunity to personally invite you to one of my upcoming seminars on Wealth Creation. I will be teaching with my friend and associate Scot Anderson, who is also an established author, business owner and successful investor. In addition to Scot and myself, we will have our team members there for you to meet. Some of my team members include specialized attorneys, mentors and tax strategists. Each of them will share the practical keys to success as it pertains to their area of expertise. This seminar is based on the real-life keys that people need to start and continue to build wealth.

In addition to this seminar, we offer a coaching program. If you're interested in obtaining information on one or both of these programs, please refer to the final pages of the book.

As we conclude this study, I want to take a moment to summarize and review what we've covered.

We began by discussing how important it is to get over your past and to realize that you have a good life. You may have gotten the impression that my family is not together or that we have a host of problems based on the past. Nothing could be further from the truth. Today, we enjoy some of the best relationships possible, including my mom and my recently reunited dad and sister. Having great relationships is not something that just happens. It's something that you choose and it's something that you work for. It's always worth it in the end. The important thing is to remember that your past is your past and nothing that ever happened to you will keep you from a great future unless you allow it to by dwelling on it.

We then discussed belief systems and how they impact every part of your life. What you really believe dictates how you will act and how you will respond to opportunities that come your way. Your belief system exercises a tremendous control over your life. It is imperative that you take the time to make sure your belief systems are consistent with the kind of life that you want to lead in every area.

Along the same lines, we saw that your thoughts are extremely important, particularly as they relate to your ability to create wealth. It's time that we think for a change. Don't think in a way that will cause you to stay the same as you've always been. Think, "change," so that you don't think the way you always have. You have the ability to decide your thoughts. Make sure that you think your thoughts. Don't let your thoughts think you. Take control of them and focus them on your future success.

We also saw how important it is to not just set traditional goals like we were taught in the past. Begin to visualize what it is that you want. Be able to see the things that you believe you will eventually have. It is also very important to know why you want things. Be clear on the whys behind your desires. This will help motivate you in your pursuit of your goals. The power of having a goal is not simply in saying that you have one, but it is in turning that goal into something that you are passionate about so that you will do what is required to achieve it. This is accomplished by never losing sight of the reasons that you set out to build wealth in the first place.

> **Be clear on the whys behind your desires.**

Your most important asset in the pursuit of your goals is your time. If you learn to control your time and decide wisely how and where you invest it, you will steadily move toward the wealth that you want. Time is the number one asset that you possess. It's not your money and it's not any other resource. Time is the one thing you can't replace. Once it's gone, you can't get it back. Use it wisely. Make sure you manage it in such a way that you are productive and successful in every area of your life.

Looking rich is expensive. We talked about how important it is for you to have a clear spending plan. It's not about having a budget where you are focused on constantly cutting costs but rather a spending plan in which you focus on increasing your cash flow. One of the keys is to understand that wealthy people are not concerned with looking rich. They are concerned with being rich. Do not get caught up in the trap of spending your money trying to look rich. All that you will have then is the appearance of being wealthy without the actual wealth. Do not increase your lifestyle until you actually have the wealth to do it. Let your wealth drive your lifestyle, not the other way around.

Becoming financially literate is vital to getting money to work for you rather than you working for money. Working for money is truly hard work and I know that you'll agree, once you've done it, you are not looking forward to doing it anymore. Getting money to work for you will not happen overnight. But it is very rewarding as you begin to see the results. To get there, you have to learn all that you can about how finances work. Become literate.

Do not just focus on the simple goal of making money. Money is a result. But it is the result of definite actions that you take. Purpose to do things that will improve your wealth. Purpose to be a problem solver. Purpose to build a team of relationships that you can lean on for advice and resources. Purpose to keep people in debt to you by always trying to benefit them. Purpose to think results. Purpose to gain mentors whom you trust and respect.

Once you have laid this foundation, we come to the most important part of the book—the Real Money, Real Time Wealth Creation System: Assess, Access, Accumulate. This is a practical, methodical system to start building wealth today and to see immediate results. You simply need to assess your current position in life, access greater cash flow and begin to accumulate wealth. No matter what your age, where you live or what kind of job you have now, anybody can begin to accumulate wealth with this system. You don't need to have money to start with. You don't need experience. All you need is to choose to start and then do it.

My two favorite ways of building wealth are building businesses and investing in real estate. There are many ways that you can accomplish these things. Starting a business doesn't require any special talents or resources. You can start right now with what you already know how to do and like to do. All you need is an idea. Become creative and turn your ideas into increased cash flow that you can use to create an investment account.

Then, it is a matter of investing for your future. I love real estate, but that isn't the only way that you can invest. Look around you for opportunities. Think outside the box. I've given you the tools to get started and the resources to ask the questions that will help you make intelligent and wise decisions about how and where to put your investments. Build your team and learn to rely on them. It will reap great benefits.

Plan—Do—Review

As you begin the process of creating wealth, not everything will turn out the way you planned. It is very important that you live by the principle of planning, doing and reviewing. Plan what it is that you believe is important to do. Execute the plan. Then take the time to review it and make sure that you are getting the results you intended. If the results aren't what you intended, then make some adjustments and try something else. The definition of insanity is doing the same thing over and over again, expecting different results. Be result minded. If the results aren't there, change something and try again.

The first money that was ever minted for the United States was a coin designed by Benjamin Franklin. It had the motto, "Mind your business" engraved on it. By that Franklin meant to pay attention to your work. That is good advice. Mind your business, watch your bottom line and look for new ways of doing things. Search for ideas. Look for coaches and mentors who have gone before you. Choose to live a life full of learning and investing in yourself. The more you learn, the more you will know for the next time. If you fail, it simply means that you have learned another way not to do it. It is a step to your future success. Eventually you will get it right.

Failure is not an option. You really only fail if you give up. Weighing the rewards versus the cost will always cause you to persist a little bit longer. Go for your dream. If you don't, no one else will. In the pursuit of your dreams, you will find satisfaction, gratification and purpose. It is only my opinion, but I believe that one of the primary reasons why people experience a midlife crisis is because they are not working towards what they've always dreamed about. One day they wake up and they realize that they're not doing what it is they always wanted to do. You may not arrive next month or next year, but if you continue on doing what is important to you, you will reach your dreams.

This brings up another point that I want to leave with you. Value your health. The more financially successful I become, the more aware and conscious I am of how important it is for me to be healthy. Without health, I will never be able to enjoy the fruits of my labor. I will never be able to enjoy taking those trips that I've always dreamed of taking or give away the money that I've always dreamed of giving. If my health is not of primary concern to me, my wealth will

If my health is not of primary concern to me, my wealth will be of no use to me.

be of no use to me. Recently, I hired a personal trainer and a personal chef who specializes in health food. One of the great advantages of building wealth is being able to do what's best for your body and for your health and for your family without ever having to think about whether or not you can afford it.

I want to encourage you to see beyond material possessions and ask yourself a far more important question. "What kind of a legacy will I leave behind?" I didn't write this book because I needed another source of income. I wrote it because I wanted to help people change their lives. By that I don't just mean changing their finances so that they can do whatever they want. Rather I want to change lives in a way that allows them to have more money so that they can affect the people closest to them in a positive way. I want to see people become better providers, better friends, better husbands and wives, better parents and better citizens. I want you to be able to affect the world you live in for the good.

When I first got started building wealth, it was all about getting my needs met. I was so desperate to make sure that I could pay my bills, and I was tired of living paycheck to paycheck. But after my needs were met and I began to realize financial success, I started to see the big picture of what wealth was really for. It was not just for me. The wealth by itself is meaningless.

Possessions just don't stand the test of time, no matter how much you take care of them. A new car will eventually become a used car and then a dilapidated car. Your new home will appreciate in value for a long time but sooner or later, it will become an old house. Relationships, family, friends and the memories that you create with them will always stand the test of time. And they will bring you more joy and satisfaction than anything you can purchase with your wealth.

One of my favorite movies of all time is Bruce Almighty. In the story, Bruce Nolan, played by Jim Carrey, is given the powers of God. He can do anything he wants to do, go anywhere he wants to go and have anything he wants to have with one exception. He does not have the power to make his girlfriend, Grace Connelly, played by Jennifer Aniston, fall in love with him. As the story progresses, he discovers that love is the only thing that really matters to him. Without the value of relationships, nothing in life is important to him anymore.

This is a great time to ask yourself the same question. What is the big picture in your life? Are you aware of what your Creator made you for? Do you understand your legacy and mission in life? It needs to be more than just making money. The goals that you set for yourself need to insure that you will always value the things that matter most in life.

I see people all the time who start off in life with no real mission for who or what they need to be. They have no idea what legacy they want to leave behind. They are short-sighted. Many athletes and movie stars become rich beyond their wildest dreams. We read about them in the tabloids. We follow their lives as they go from one bad marriage to another, one broken relationship to another. They struggle with substance abuse and all kinds of problems. As I said before, money is neutral. It is not going to change you at all. It's just going to give you the ability to become even more of what you already are. If that isn't healthy, then you'd better ask yourself where you are going and make appropriate changes. Ask yourself these questions now.

Life is relatively short. So what matters to you in the end? When people are on their deathbeds, they're not wondering how great it would be if they could have earned more money or if they could have gotten one more house or started one more business. No, they're wondering about what was really important in life—their relationships, their kids and their legacy.

Having financial abundance beyond my wildest dreams means absolutely nothing to me if I don't have the people closest to me to enjoy it with. Those are questions that you will have to answer for yourself. If you ask them now, then you will be able to look back on a great life with no regrets.

I consider it an honor that you completed my book. I appreciate that you purchased it and that you took the time to read it. I am more excited, though, about the results that it will have in your life. Creating wealth is fun and I hope that you will join me in making a difference for others around you. I look forward to personally meeting you at some point in life, perhaps at our next seminar. Until then, keep working towards your dreams and I'll see you at the top!

GET YOUR 3 FREE SPECIAL GIFTS FROM JOHN

10 Keys to Being Liked Instantly

A Guide to Create and Operate Multiple Businesses

Top 3 business opportunities capable of producing $10,000 per month profit within 90 days! These have all been personally tried and proven by either John or one of his business partners.
(Individual results may vary)

Send an email to:

wealthppl@cox.net

to request your three gifts.

Would you like to have John speak at your next corporate function, conference, church, or school?

John will carefully customize his talk for you and your audience. Call today for full information on booking John to speak at your next meeting or conference.

For further information please send an email to:

wealthppl@cox.net

or an invitation to:

John Hrimnak
PO Box 10549
Scottsdale AZ 85271-0549

Live Events Coming to Your Area

***ACTIVATE* your dream**   ***DOMINATE* your life**

***INCREASE* your cash flow**   ***MULTIPLY* your wealth**

I look forward to meeting you at one of my upcoming wealth building seminars. For more information, please visit:

www.richnowrichforlife.com

VIP ADMISSION TICKET

Present this ticket to receive admission for two to see John live at an upcoming ACTIVATE your Wealth seminar coming to your city. This is a total value of $300! Visit www.richnowrichforlife.com for dates and locations. RSVP to richforlife@cox.net.

Live Coaching and Seminars

We offer a variety of programs created to assist you in the process of creating wealth.

The various coaching models ensure that you are on track with achieving your goals. Our seminars will provide you with an intense wealth-building experience. Our goal is to provide you with the practical tools to begin creating additional wealth. At our seminars, you will have the opportunity to design your own wealth creation plan, meet members of my wealth team and realize key principles to success. We are so convinced that our seminar will be of value to you that we provide a unique, no questions asked money-back guarantee. Everything that we do is designed to methodically and practically help people live the life of which they've always dreamed. I'm looking forward to joining your team!

Special Offer

If you are traveling from out of state to attend our seminar, you will receive one complimentary admission for every one you purchase. Single mothers with children under eighteen years old receive a half-price admission.

For further information on all our programs, including personal coaching or additional online resources, visit us at:

Breakingthewealthcode.com

TAKE THE
BREAKING THE WEALTH CODE CHALLENGE

Join me in making a difference in the world we live in by joining "**The Breaking the Wealth Code Challenge.**"

We want to record the number of people experiencing results using our system by increasing their monthly income by a minimum of 10%. Imagine the difference any amount of additional income would make in your own life. I know for me, starting out, it was the difference between night and day. Start with yourself and then tell others about the:

Real Money, Real Time Wealth Creation System

I believe as we are able to help individuals and families start with accomplishing this goal, it helps to improve every area of their lives, directly affecting those closest to them in a positive way. I truly believe this additional income will help our economy through increased consumer spending and job creation. The creation of disposable spending would also cause people to be generous in their charitable contributions, rendering much needed support and improving the world as we know it. Imagine a world in which national poverty statistics, world hunger and medical research, to name a few, are all positively impacted as a result. I believe it's possible, and it starts with you and me.

As you are experiencing results, visit our website and keep us updated. It's possible that you may be asked at some point to grant us permission to include your story in an upcoming book or seminar. Experiencing this additional income and placing it in the right investment categories will help to ensure you're on the path to wealth creation.

To share your results
or for additional information,
visit us at:

Breakingthewealthcode.com